Your Towns and Cities in th

# Gloucester
## in the Great War

Your Towns and Cities in the Great War

# Gloucester
## in the Great War

**Derek Tait**

Pen & Sword
**MILITARY**

First published in Great Britain in 2016 by
PEN & SWORD MILITARY
an imprint of
Pen and Sword Books Ltd
47 Church Street
Barnsley
South Yorkshire S70 2AS

ISBN 978 1 47382 807 0

Printed and bound in England
by CPI Group (UK) Ltd, Croydon, CR0 4YY

Typeset in Times New Roman

Pen & Sword Books Ltd incorporates the imprints of
Pen & Sword Archaeology, Atlas, Aviation, Battleground, Discovery,
Family History, History, Maritime, Military, Naval, Politics, Railways,
Select, Social History, Transport, True Crime, and Claymore Press,
Frontline Books, Leo Cooper, Praetorian Press, Remember When,
Seaforth Publishing and Wharncliffe.
For a complete list of Pen and Sword titles please contact
Pen and Sword Books Limited
47 Church Street, Barnsley, South Yorkshire, S70 2AS, England
E-mail: enquiries@pen-and-sword.co.uk
Website: **www.pen-and-sword.co.uk**

# Contents

# Acknowledgements

Thanks to Norman (Flickr), Paul Pearson, Daisy Parker, Derek Parker, Benjamin Pile, Alan Tait, Ellen Tait, Tina Cole and Tilly Barker. Thanks also to the helpful and friendly team at Pen and Sword, including Roni Wilkinson, Matt Jones, Jon Wilkinson, Diane Wordsworth, Katie Eaton, Laura Lawton and Jodie Butterwood.

# Newspapers

*The Birmingham Daily Post*
*The Cheltenham Chronicle*
*The Citizen*
*The Evening Herald*
*The Gloucester Journal*
*The Montana Yellowstone News*
*The Western Times*

*Chapter One*

# 1914 – Eager for a Fight

Rising tensions in Europe and the assassination of Franz Ferdinand in Sarajevo led to Austria-Hungary's declaration of war on Serbia. This led to the Central Powers, which included Germany and Austria-Hungary, and the Allies, which included the British Empire, the French Republic and the Russian Empire, to declare war on each other, which led to the commencement of the First World War on 28 July 1914.

On 4 August, newspaper offices posted announcements in their windows stating that Britain had declared war on Germany.

People of foreign descent were quickly rounded up and detained. Anyone with a German-sounding accent soon came under suspicion of being a spy.

The railways were taken under government control under the Regulations of Forces Act of 1871. Local businesses were asked to supply motor vehicles for use by the army, and businesses in and around Gloucester were asked to supply horses.

**Archduke Franz Ferdinand of Austria. Ferdinand's assassination in Sarajevo on 28 June 1914 led to Austria-Hungary's declaration of war on Serbia, which ultimately led to the beginning of the First World War.**

**Kitchener's recruitment poster, 'Your country needs you!' A huge recruitment campaign encouraged young men to join-up. By January 1915, almost 1,000,000 men had enlisted. Pals battalions encouraged many to enlist and they ultimately provided enough men for three battalions.**

**A pre-war photo showing the 1st/6th Gloucesters on their way to Perham Down on the edge of Salisbury Plain.**

On 6 August, HMS *Amphion*, a Devonport-based cruiser, became the first Royal Navy casualty of the war.

On the previous day, *Amphion* and the 3rd Flotilla received a report from a trawler that a ship had been spotted 'throwing things overboard'. The trawler gave the ship's position, and *Amphion* and the flotilla set off to investigate. Soon after, they spotted the minelayer SMS *Königin Luise* heading eastwards. *Königin Luise* was a German-requisitioned former Hamburg-Netherlands holiday ferry that had been converted into an auxiliary minelayer.

On the evening of 4 August, she had left Emden on a course for the North Sea with the intent of laying mines off the Thames Estuary. *Königin Luise* was disguised in the colours of steamers of the Great Eastern Railway, which were black, buff and yellow. The genuine steamers travelled from Harwich to the Hook of Holland.

*Königin Luise's* attempt to escape aroused suspicions from the approaching fleet, and four destroyers, including *Landrail* and *Lance*, gave chase. Within the hour, *Königin Luise* was sunk. From a crew of

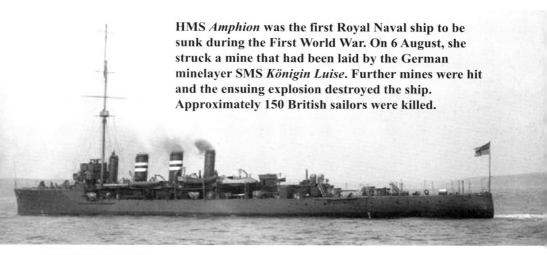

HMS *Amphion* was the first Royal Naval ship to be sunk during the First World War. On 6 August, she struck a mine that had been laid by the German minelayer SMS *Königin Luise*. Further mines were hit and the ensuing explosion destroyed the ship. Approximately 150 British sailors were killed.

Kitchener's call to arms. The great numbers of men needed for the army were brought together by regular appeals by the authorities for young men to join-up. The campaign went on around the country. This photo shows a recruitment speaker surrounded by flags and posters. On the chairs are the various uniforms of the army and the speaker is compelling young men to put one on rather than wearing civilian attire.

100 there were forty-six survivors, and *Amphion* picked up many of these before continuing on her pre-arranged search of the waters.

The destroyers soon located another ship of the same shape and colour as the *Königin Luise*, this time flying a large German flag. The destroyers opened fire on the ship. However, *Amphion* realised that the ship was in fact the *St Petersburg*. On board was the German Ambassador returning to Germany from England. *Amphion* signalled to the destroyers to cease fire but they continued, at which point *Amphion* positioned itself between the destroyers and the *St Petersburg*, which allowed the ship to continue on its journey safely.

They continued to search the waters until 3.30am on 6 August when they began their return to Harwich. However, their return course ran close to where *Königin Luise* had placed mines and at 6.30 am, *Amphion* struck one of these mines, killing many men aboard, while also incapacitating the captain. When the captain recovered, he ran to the engine room to shut down the engines. The vessel's back was already broken and the escorting destroyers returned to rescue *Amphion*'s crew. At the same time they rescued several German survivors. Although the engines had been shut down, *Amphion* continued to drift towards the minefield and at 7.30 am struck a row of mines, which shot debris over the rescue boats and destroyers. A shell from *Amphion* hit the deck of *Lark* killing two of *Amphion*'s rescued crew as well as a German prisoner. *Amphion* sank within fifteen minutes of the last explosion. Almost 150 British sailors were killed, as well as eighteen of the crew rescued from *Königin Luise*.

Thomas Webb and Reginald Gill, both members of respected families in Gloucester, survived the ordeal. The *Cheltenham Chronicle* noted of Webb and Gill: 'They are to be congratulated upon being saved from a perilous situation. Both are quite young, the one being a stoker and the other an A.B.'

The seriousness of the war wasn't instantly appreciated by many, as the *Cheltenham Chronicle* of Saturday, 8 August reported:

> *Of course, the all absorbing theme is the Great War, but a number of townsfolk did not seem to realise the gravity of the situation up to Saturday night. Local interest began to show itself, however, some twenty-four hours later and excitement has been on the increase. An excited crowd waited up on Tuesday night to try to glean news relating to our final ultimatum.*

The newspaper went on to report under the headline 'This week at Gloucester':

A female shell worker. During the war,
900,000 women were employed in
munition factories. Volunteers came
from all social classes and the work was
said to be hard as well as dangerous.

*With the declaration of war on Germany by France, with the dragging of England and other powers into the conflict through what has been appropriately described as the unreasonable and high-handed policy of the Kaiser and his advisers, nothing but war has been talked of during the week and events, which in time of peace would have claimed the attention of the public, have been dismissed with a passing thought. The mobilisation and departure of the Territorials created a good deal of excitement, the city being crowded with people from the commencement of the assembling of the men until their departure at night. As the men marched to the railway station, considerable enthusiasm prevailed but there were none of those mafficking scenes which characterised the departure*

**A horse being loaded on board ship. Hundreds of thousands of horses were requisitioned during the war and many died in combat. Some, however, did survive and were brought back to Britain, and a few were cared for by animal charities.**

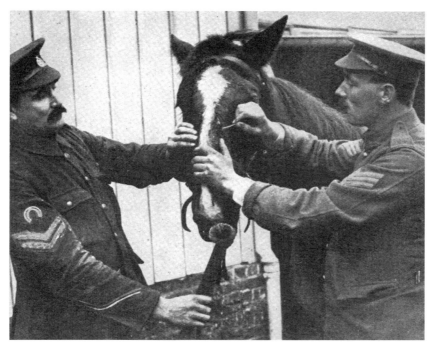

**Two soldiers take care of one of their horses. Casualties amongst horses in the artillery and transport divisions were high but soldiers of the Army Veterinary Corps worked hard to relieve any suffering. All wounds and injuries were carefully treated. Here, a sergeant sews up a wound on a horse's nose.**

*of the Reservists and Territorials at the time of the Boer War. The general public appeared to realise the seriousness of the occasion and refrained from indulging in licentious behaviour. Now our men have left to fight for their country, it is to be hoped that the excellent appeal made by the Mayor to the citizens, will be acted upon by those left behind. His Worship, after assuring those who have left their homes to defend their country that their wives and families will be looked after by the citizens, especially appealed to employers to keep open the places of those called away. The latter appeal is very desirable, when it is remembered that a large number of Reservists who were called out in the Boer War found their places filled on returning home and were out of work for a considerable period.*

Horses fared badly at the Front. Many were killed by artillery fire and were affected by skin conditions and poison gas. Hundreds of thousands of horses died during the conflict. Many horses were requisitioned from

**Many men rush to enlist, 1914. As war was announced, men of all ages were keen to enlist and showed much patriotism. Many saw it as an adventure, a way to escape unemployment or their humdrum daily lives. Most thought that the war wouldn't last long and would be over by Christmas.**

British civilians. However, Lord Kitchener stated that no horse under 15 hands should be confiscated. This was because many children showed a concern about the welfare of their ponies.

The *Cheltenham Chronicle* of Saturday, 15 August reported:

*In connection with most other towns, the week at Gloucester has been marked by the hurrying to and from of Territorials. The past week-end saw the local battery of the Field Artillery entrain for the south and, in the beginning of the present week, the street resounded to the tramp of horses' hoofs as the A, and part of C, Squadrons of the Royal Gloucestershire Hussars gathered together their mounts and transport vehicles preparatory to reporting themselves at their headquarters on Tuesday. Each of the units had a hearty send-off by the citizens, who have come to regard their local soldiers in a more serious light than before the outbreak of the war.*

The first shots by British troops on foreign soil took place on 21 August 1914. A military unit of the 4th Dragoon Guards, comprising 120 men, was sent on a reconnoitre mission ahead of the British Expeditionary

Force. Although members of the British Expeditionary Force had landed a week before, no contact with the enemy had taken place. As forces advanced into France and Belgium, they heard stories from civilians that large numbers of German troops were advancing towards the town of Mons in Belgium. Shortly after, the cavalry men of the Dragoon Guards encountered the enemy and the first shots taken in Europe by British troops since the Battle of Waterloo became the first of millions to be fired over the next four years.

On Wednesday, 26 August, Major General Jeffreys, the inspector of recruiting, addressed a meeting at the Guildhall, which was attended by employers and prominent citizens of Gloucester. The aim of the meeting was to stimulate recruitment in the city and surrounding area. It was suggested that sub-committees be formed so they could canvas different wards within the community, appealing to young men to enlist.

Captain Allen stated that new recruits had been enlisting daily and that 682 had joined from the northern part of the county. The number of recruits from Gloucester totalled 200.

**Women making bandages for injured troops. While their menfolk were away fighting, many women found themselves on the Home Front employed in useful tasks, such as nursing, factory work, shell-making and agricultural work.**

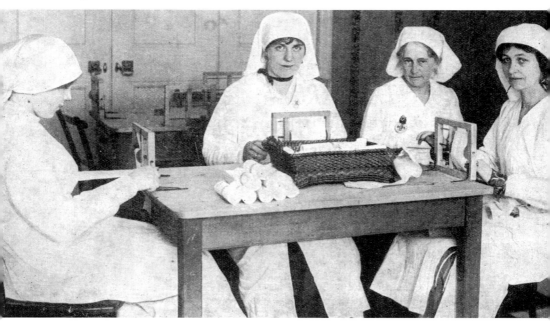

**Wounded troops returning from France in 1914. When the first wounded troops arrived on English soil from France, they were able to tell people about the war as it really was. It was said that anyone who met one of the wounded soldiers would never forget the emotions that it aroused.**

Towards the end of August, thirty men from the Atlas Iron Works, belonging to Messrs Fielding and Platt, enlisted in the army in a 24-hour period. A further forty had enlisted on the previous Friday morning. The firm guaranteed that the wives of young married men would receive 10 shillings a week from the firm to supplement army pay and separation allowances. Meanwhile, at Messrs W. Butler and Co's works at Upper Parting, a notice was issued, which read:

*Any man in our employ, already serving with the colours, or wishing to volunteer, will have his situation kept open for him until his return at the end of the war. The company will see that the wives, families or dependants of these men shall be in no worse position than if the men were at work.*

The *Gloucester Journal* of Saturday, 29 August reported on a case involving the restriction of aliens. The article read:

> At Gloucester City Petty Sessions on Monday – before the Mayor (Mr James Bruton), in the chair and other magistrates – the two German seamen Emil Willy Arthur Scholz and Rudy Zerries, who on the previous Monday were remanded in order that the police might communicate with the Home Office, were again placed in the dock to be dealt with. It will be remembered that the prisoners practically gave themselves up at the Gloucester police station on the evening of August 13th.
>
> The magistrates' clerk (Mr Frank Treasure) said the prisoners were the persons charged the previous Monday with being German subjects landing in a prohibited port, contrary to the Aliens Restrictions Act, 1914. Communications had been received from the Secretary of State for the Home Department, pointing out that the magistrates, before handing prisoners over to the military authorities, should deal with them in the terms of the Privy Council Order and either impose a term of imprisonment or fine them up to £100. It was then for the police to decide whether or not they should arrest prisoners as dangerous subjects or allow them to go on registering themselves as aliens.

**Recruits going to the station on Tuesday, 1 September 1914. A large number of men enlisted at the Shire Hall and nearby army barracks, the two main recruiting centres, on the outbreak of war. The new recruits were cheered as they made their way to the train station, where the mayor wished them 'God-speed and a safe return'.**

The new recruits leaving Gloucester by train on their way to camp on 1 September 1914. There was a large crowd of well-wishers at the station and the train steamed out amid a scene of great enthusiasm.

*The Mayor said the justices had gone into the case very carefully before entering the court and had decided not to send prisoners to gaol but to inflict a fine of £2 10s on each of them. They would then, on signing the register as aliens, be allowed to go if the police made no objection.*

*Mr Robert Dion Jeune, who again acted as interpreter, conveyed the Justices' decision to the prisoners. He was thanked by the Mayor, on behalf of the bench and the police, for his services throughout the case.*

An advert for Blinkhorn's of Gloucester, who supplied Red Cross outfits for nurses treating wounded soldiers within the city's hospitals. Saturday, 5 September 1914.

On Wednesday, 9 September, the *Birmingham Daily Post* reported the departure of Gloucester recruits for 'Kitchener's Army'. The article read:

> *Another contingent of 189 recruits for Lord Kitchener's Army left Gloucester yesterday, and like those who had gone before, they were given an enthusiastic send-off. Addressing the men at the Shire Hall, the Mayor (Councillor James Bruton) stated that the number departing that day made a total of 1,300 recruits for Lord Kitchener's Army from the city of Gloucester alone, which was a splendid record.*
>
> *This number did not, however, represent all the men who had departed from their midst, for if they took into consideration those who had left to enlist or to take their places in the Navy, territorials, Yeomanry and the Royal Field Artillery, it would be found that close upon 3,000 men had gone from Gloucester to serve with the colours. The Gloucesters being full up, the present contingent was going to join the Worcesters.*
>
> *Over 160 recruits have been obtained to supply wastage in the 5th Battalion Gloucester Regiment.*

The *Cheltenham Chronicle* of Saturday, 19 September congratulated the Gloucestershire Root, Fruit and Grain Society for carrying on with their annual show, scheduled for 9 November. The newspaper wrote:

> *It passes understanding why some people wish everything put off during the present troublous times. The war itself makes men and things gloomy enough and the abandoning of functions such as an agricultural produce show would simply make matters in this direction much worse. I fail to see*

**Tom Wiltshire joined the Gloucestershire Regiment in Bristol on 8 September 1914, age 24, from the Territorials, and served throughout the Great War in the 1st/6th Battalion. He saw active service in France, Flanders and Italy, serving as Private 265783. He survived the war and died in 1962, age 72.**

*what arguments can be used in support of preventing members exhibiting the produce of the land. Whatever other businesses have to be suspended, the tilling of the land must of necessity continue, and when we bear in mind that the one great anxiety of those in authority is to increase, in every possible way, the cultivation of food for the people, there can surely be no reasonable objection to the holding of the exhibition.*

During September, John Stevens, a farmer, was charged with cruelty towards a horse while working it at Gloucester earlier in the month.

Deputy Chief Constable William Harrison and PC Yates both stated that Stevens had used the horse to bring a cargo of fruit to Gloucester Market and, on examination of the horse, the constable found that the animal had two running sores on its shoulder, which were old scars where the harness had rubbed it raw. The defendant said that the horse had been all right when it left home but admitted the harness was hard and immediately bought a new one. He stated that only two days before, the army had examined the horse and would have taken it away had it been two inches taller. The defendant also said he was a paid up member to the Society for the Prevention of Cruelty to Animals. The case was dismissed on payment of costs.

**Jack Judge, the composer of It's a Long Way to Tipperary. The song was bought by British music publisher, Feldman, for £5 and became a favourite with the troops. Judge's family were Irish and his grandparents had originally come from Tipperary. The song was recorded by John McCormack in 1914 and soon became popular all around the world.**

At the same court hearings, Thomas Ramsey was accused of stealing a bicycle with a value of £3 10s. The case was adjourned for a week to give the accused, who was previously in the army, a chance to rejoin the colours. DCC Harrison stated in court that he had been in telephonic communication with his commanding officer at Horfield, who stated that Ramsay had twice deserted and they would not accept him in the army again. Ramsay was sent to prison for fourteen days.

John Higgins, who was apprehended by Detective Coles on 11 September, admitted being a deserter from his Majesty's Army Corps at Aldershot and was remanded in custody to await an escort back.

Towards the end of September, the *Cheltenham Chronicle* reported that recruitment for the Fifth Gloucesters was still proceeding, although the requisite number of men required would soon be obtained. The men already enlisted were said to have had a very busy week.

The 1st Gloucestershire Regiment at Bordon, Hampshire, 1914. The Gloucestershire Regiment fought on the Western Front and at Gallipoli, Mesopotamia, Macedonia, Persia and Italy. Altogether, twenty-five battalions were raised and included many men from Gloucester as well as from other parts of Great Britain.

Wives wave off their loved ones as sailors leave on board a train. Most travelled third-class, and two men can be seen with pipes in the special 'smoking' carriage.

**Cyclists on Foreign Service Parade. The 5th Gloucesters took part in a cross-country race at Chelmsford during October 1914, which resulted in a win for G Company. A pair of socks, presented by the queen, was given to all competitors who finished the course. The overall winner of the race, named only as 'Knight', received a medal and £1.**

After assembling each day at the barracks at 6.30 am, they remained on duty, with intervals for breakfast and dinner, until 4.30 pm. A route march had taken place, which covered 9 miles and lasted 2½ hours. Four

**The 5th Gloucesters at Chelmsford during October 1914. The photo shows some of the competitors taking part in the Battalion Sports as well as members of their regiments. Well-known Gloucester athletes were among the group, including S. Smart, an international, who came second in the cross-country race. His prize was 10 shillings.**

**The 5th Gloucesters at Chelmsford, from the *Gloucester Journal* of Saturday, 10 October 1914. The picture shows a party of trench diggers who attended the inter-company cross-country race.**

men were unable to complete the march, although the same discipline applied to new recruits as to regular members of the army. Half-a-dozen men were late for the early drill and their punishment involved marching around the barrack square for an hour at night.

On Saturday, 17 October, the *Cheltenham Chronicle* reported about the refugee situation in the city:

*The first official party of the large number of Belgian refugees which may be expected in Gloucester have arrived. Although their prospects are anything but bright, and they have probably lost everything but the few odds and ends of clothes rescued from the devastation of war, they appeared to accept their fate with resignation and to be thankful for the hospitality afforded them by the old city. Already we have some 50 refugees amongst us and, in the course of a week or so, may expect another 80. The first party, numbering 10, have been housed in Nettleton Road and others will be accommodated at*

**Lieutenant C.A.S. Carleton was reported wounded in the *Gloucester Journal* of Saturday; 10 October 1914. He had been educated at the Crypt Grammar School in Gloucester and was well-known in the city. He also played football for Gloucester for two seasons.**

**An advert for Beecham's Pills which featured in the *Gloucester Journal* of Saturday, 10 October 1914.**

**The 4th Gloucesters on the Bristol Grammar School Playing Field, Tyndall's Park. The 2nd Company are in the foreground. The officers shown are Lieutenant Holloway and Lieutenant Irving.**

*Newark House, Hempsted, a large residence lying back from the road and affording the quiet rest necessary after the turmoil of flight from a country overrun by enemies.*

Also on 17 October, a letter appeared in the *Gloucester Journal* from Lieutenant Colonel A.C. Lovett of the 28th Gloucestershire Regiment. It was headed 'In the trenches, France'. In the letter he stated that his men were cheerful and in good health and they wished to express their gratitude for all the gifts they had received, which included tobacco, pipes and other luxuries. He said the men were stimulated to carry out their duties knowing that many back home were thinking of them. He requested that now the weather was getting colder, that people send woollen scarves and gloves (in khaki or brown colour) and warm vests. However, he finished by saying that tobacco was most prized among the men.

Later in October, a letter was received at the Gloucester police station from former PC Frank Smith, who was serving with the 2nd Welsh Regiment as part of the Expeditionary Force. In

**The wife of Private J. Hopkins, of 55 Napier Street, Gloucester, received notification from the War Office of her husband's death during October 1914. He had served with the 2nd Welsh Regiment and was killed in action on 14 September 1914. Private Hopkins had been a reservist and had previously worked as a lamplighter with the Gloucester Gas Company. His widow was left with four children.**

**Injured troops prepare to return home. In the first year of the war there were very few hospital trains equipped for the needs of wounded soldiers. Third-class trains were used, and wounded and gassed soldiers had to sit upright on the long journey. Special hospital trains were later introduced.**

the letter he said he was quite well and had, up to the present, been quite successful in dodging bullets. He went on to say that he was well-fed but that all the men could do with more 'smokes', and said that currently they were given one cigarette between two men. He concluded his letter with, 'Tell the cook I shall be back for the Christmas dinner.'

*The Gloucester Journal* of 31 October carried a letter from a mother to another mother of a son lost in the war:

*We reported recently that Mrs Morgan, 6 Baker Street, Gloucester, had received an intimation from the War Office that her son, 16292 Private G. Morgan, 2nd Batt. Grenadier Guards, had been killed in action. Mrs Morgan, who has another son in the 1st Gloucesters*

**Walking wounded and bedraggled troops wait to board a train to take them to hospital. All are dishevelled and dirty from fighting at the Front. Carriages in the background are packed with soldiers taking a break for refreshments before returning to a rest camp.**

*with the Expeditionary Force in France, has since received the following letter:*

*Dear Madam,*

*May I, as the mother of a young officer in the same Battalion of Grenadiers as your son, write to you some of the sympathy which*

*as a mother I can feel for you now. My son, who is only 21 and a Lieutenant, wrote to me two days after your son was killed and he was evidently so fond of him that I felt I must tell you what he said. I will quote his words:*

*'There are many tragic moments. Here is one. Latterly, the Germans for some reason have not been shelling our trenches so heavily as usual. Two afternoons ago, the men's teas were brought up. No shelling whatsoever was going on. Obviously the Germans saw the men coming because they were not taking quite such precautions as usual to avoid being seen, for hardly had we started*

*to issue the teas than the Germans began to shell us. We all went under the shelter directly and I hoped that no-one had been touched but in an interval, I went out with a couple of men to look round and, in a part of the trench leading from one point to another, I found one of the men – Morgan. He had been killed on the spot I'm sure. He was a splendid fellow, a great big man. He died happy I think, for only that day he had had a parcel of matches and cigarettes from home and had been so pleased giving them to his pals.'*

*My son then goes on to say:*

*'One more thing I must tell you about him. On one other occasion, before I came out, the Germans shelled and set on fire a house which had about 60 or 80 German prisoners in it. Morgan was one of those who helped to get them out. He brought them out, one under each arm, I believe. When he got back late to the company that night, and was asked why he was late, he said that he had stayed behind to let out the cows, who were being burned, as he was fond of animals. All this was under shell fire.'*

*This is what my son says and I know to me it would be happiness to know that any small parcel I had sent could have reached and given him so much pleasure; and oh! how proud your poor, sad heart must be of such a son, who could be so brave and yet so humble in his bravery. His death is one of the glorious things of this terrible war and the sorrow is all yours. He was happy and went from this world in the full enjoyment of his life. May God help you to bear your mother's sorrow. I hope what I have been able to tell you will have lightened it a little. I expect his parcel was from you, so yours was the hand that gave him his happy day.*

*Your friend in anxiety,*
*Helen Beaumont Nesbitt.*

At the Palace Theatre, commencing 31 October, Messrs Poole put on a production portraying the events of the war so far. Artists worked day and night to paint the scenery. The show featured scenes of battle, which were said to be incredibly realistic, with the *Gloucester Journal* describing the performance as 'wonderful' and 'the greatest pitch of perfection'. The production included patriotic songs, a comedian – Wee Wilkins (Bristol's own baby comedian) – and Reg Maurice, a lightning cartoonist.

On Monday, 2 November, the mayor and mayoress made a visit to the Red Cross Hospital in Great Western Road. They chatted freely with the wounded British and Belgian soldiers and Mrs Bruton gave each soldier a box of chocolates, which were much appreciated by the men.

On Thursday, 5 November, Mrs Staines, who had become known locally as 'the lady with the bucket', was allowed by the Palladium to collect funds outside the theatre. The amount collected totalled £2 10s. She had previously collected a further 10s at a matinee on 22 October. Altogether, to date, she collected £41 9s 10d and appealed to other venues to allow her to collect outside. The funds were raised to help Belgian war refugees.

A report in the *Gloucester Journal* of Saturday, 7 November, announced that eight wounded British and two wounded Belgian soldiers had arrived in the city, bound for the Gloucester Red Cross Hospital. The soldiers had arrived by train at 8.50 pm. The commandant of the hospital had been expecting thirty-two wounded, but when the train arrived there were only ten on board. They were met at the station by a squad of St John's Ambulance men with a detachment of Red Cross nurses. All cases were said to be not of a serious nature and all men were able to sit up in bed. Due to the short notice given of the men arriving, few local people turned up to welcome them. Motor cars were laid on by the commandants of the hospital, Mrs Lee Williams, Miss Evans and Dr Terry. Additional cars were supplied by Mr Garbutt of the Cross Garage. Mr Watts, one of the quartermasters at the Red Cross Hospital, said: 'All the men are as keen as mustard to get back to the trenches.' Some of them had suggested running up Robinshood Hill to get fit again.

**Second Lieutenant Harold E. Hippisley, of the Gloucester Regiment, was killed in action in November 1914. He was a native of Wells and was formerly a student at the Royal Agricultural College at Cirencester. He was also a well-known cricket and hockey player in Gloucestershire and Somerset. On the day that his regiment sailed, he married Miss Ivy Hussey Cooper of Southsea.**

A letter was sent from the crew of HMS *Gloucester* to the Gloucester Chamber of Commerce on 14 November. It read:

*Dear Sir,*

*Will you kindly express to the President and members of the*

**The Gloucester Regiment at camp. Tom Wiltshire is seen in the front row on the left of the picture.**

*Gloucester Chamber of Commerce the grateful thanks of the ship's company of this ship for the plum puddings you have so kindly sent?*

*You may be sure that when the time comes for their consumption many kind thoughts and good wishes will be expressed for those who had the happy idea of sharing their Christmas dinners with those at sea.*

*We also wish to thank you personally for all the trouble you have given yourself and the interest you have taken in this much appreciated gift.*

*The packages are safely to hand.*

*Yours very truly,*
*H. Kelly.*
*Captain.*

Also on 14 November, the *Gloucester Journal* published two letters from wounded soldiers, recuperating in England. The first was received by Mrs Speck of 75 Alfred Street and came from her son, Frank W. Speck, of the 1st Gloucesters. He wrote from his hospital bed in Sunderland:

*Just a line to let you know that I am in the land of the living, though not feeling very fit. I was wounded on 23rd of last month in the trenches between Langemark and Dixmude in Belgium, where we had a terribly hot time of it. I got shot in the neck, the bullet coming out of the back near the spine. The doctors say I have had a narrow shave. We had been fighting hard all day when I got hit. The Germans were 50 or 60 yards from us, and we thought it was all up, but our fire was too hot for them. I hope to be out of hospital soon and do a bit more but I am afraid I shall not be fit for any more fighting as the bullet touched my lung and affected my back and chest. I was bleeding a long time before I was aware of it.*

The second letter came from Trooper Gilbert Hopkins, of the 1st Lifeguards, and was sent to his parents, Mr and Mrs A.F. Hopkins of 81 Vauxhall Road. Trooper Hopkins wrote:

*We had a bayonet charge the other night. The Germans came right up to the trench which we were lying in and then they gave us the chance we had been waiting for and, my God, didn't we hammer them! The French said they buried 700 Germans and we only had six men killed and about nine wounded. I don't think they will last much longer now as there is a big battle on now which I think is their last stand before we get into Germany. I had my first experience of those 'coal-boxes'; they make a hole in the ground big enough to bury a limber wagon in.*

Private W.H. Smith of Churchdown was killed in action on 23 October 1914. He was part of the 1st Gloucester Regiment. The *Gloucester Journal* wrote in its pages: 'Deep sympathy is felt for Mr and Mrs Smith who are greatly respected in Churchtown. Since the war started, three other sons have the Colours. One is now training in the 5th Reserve Battalion of the Gloucestershire Regiment at Gloucester and the other two are in the Royal Engineers.'

On 21 November, the *Gloucester Journal* reported on a meeting of the War Relief Committee:

*A meeting of the City of Gloucester War Relief Committee was held on Wednesday, the Mayor presiding and an Inspector of the Local Government Board being present.*

A military rugby football match between the 5th Gloucesters and the Canadians during December 1914. Commenting on the big victory of the 5th Gloucesters over the Canadians at Queen's Club, it was noted in the *Gloucester Journal* that: 'the Colonials, with the exception of Sergeant Major Adams, who was an old International, had no player of outstanding notoriety, but the Gloucesters had a whole galaxy of talent. The men from Gloucester, once they had scored, did little else. The Canadians appeared tired, perhaps their journey after many camp discomforts had left them listless.' The final result, in favour of the Gloucesters, was 5 goals and 8 tries to nil.

*Reports were received as to the present condition of employment in the city showing, up to the present, there was no distress among men in consequence to the war but that some women, such as dressmakers, typists, charwomen etc., were out of employment and others only employed part time. On the suggestion of a committee appointed at a meeting convened by the Mayoress and held on 16th September last, a sub-committee was appointed to consider the question of providing work for women temporarily thrown out of employment as a consequence of the war and to manage any schemes of employment for women which may be approved by the Central Committee on Women's Employment.*

*The Mayor reported that the subscriptions paid and promised in response to his appeal in support of the Prince of Wales' National Relief Fund had reached £6,000, and that his appeal for the Belgian Relief Fund had resulted in subscriptions amounting to*

*£694, and proposals for increasing those funds were under consideration. Questions having been asked about collections being made in the public streets, it was explained that several persons had made systematic collections which had brought in considerable sums in aid of the funds but the committee considered that street collections should not be made without their approval and that it was particularly undesirable that children should be employed making collections either in the streets or from house to house.*

On Sunday, 20 December, a concert was given at the Palladium in aid of the Red Cross Society. Songs were sung by Miss Beatrice Cook, Miss Muriel Harman, Miss Parsons and Messrs Yorke, Bailey and H. Marshall. Miss Clayton gave recitations and selections were played by Miss Mabel Winfield and the Palladium Band.

Gifts from children in America arrived in Gloucester on Monday, 21 December, and were unpacked at the Shire Hall the next day. Two of the three cases were labelled 'Belgian' and were intended specifically for Belgian refugees living within the city. The items where unpacked in the committee room and contained a mixture of clothes, toys, sweets and preserved fruits. There were also many pairs of boots. Some gifts included cheery letters from the donors, including one long missive written in the Flemish language. Altogether, there were 375 gifts and, with

A notice in the *Gloucester Journal* of Saturday, 19 December 1914 requested that men inform their employers of their interest to support the Empire by enlisting in the army.

there only being 300 Belgian children in the county, there was plenty to go around. The goods were divided into twenty lots, which were to be distributed around Gloucestershire. The third case was unpacked at the library by Miss Curtis-Hayward and Miss Grenside. The gifts were intended for British children who had been made orphans due to the loss of their fathers fighting overseas. The gifts were made up mainly of

**Christmas at the Front, 1914. British soldiers found many a sprig of mistletoe amongst the apple trees spread throughout the orchards of France. Here, the troops celebrate on top of a captured German gun.**

clothes and numbered about 200.

While troops celebrated Christmas in the trenches, entertainment carried on as normal in the city. The yearly pantomime was announced on 26 December and featured the ever-popular *Cinderella*. The production, performed

**A soldier receives a Christmas gift from home. Many soldiers received a special Christmas gift from the HRH Princess Mary's Gift Fund during Christmas 1914. Here, a corporal receives a parcel containing cigarettes and tobacco. Throughout the war, families sent regular packages to their troops at the Front, which included food and clothing.**

Delivery of Christmas Fund gifts, 1914. Christmas gifts meant a lot to the men at the Front and many were sent to the troops overseas from Britain. Here, members of the Army Veterinary Corps are seen receiving their share.

Christmas 1914, complete with Christmas tree and cards. The king and queen requested that all men serving abroad should receive a Christmas card from them and the photo shows them being handed out. In the background is a makeshift Christmas tree decorated with whatever could be found.

**A soldier receives letters and parcels from home. Troops were much cheered by parcels of gifts from home, which contained cakes 'that mother made', hand-knitted socks, which were said to be much better than the army issue ones, and 'fags', which were much prized.**

at the Palace Theatre, starred well-liked comedian Jack Mackenzie, who hailed from Gloucester and had a big following in the city. Supporting him was a first-class London company, which included Miss Viola Rene as Cinderella, Tina Franks as Prince Charming and Edie Day as Dandini. The show started on Boxing Day and continued until January 1915. Special shows were laid on just for soldiers.

**Troops on board a train in France in 1914. In the early days of the war, much strain was put on the railway service in France as every bit of rolling stock was brought into use for the transportation of troops. The carriage shown is marked '8 horses and 32 to 40 men', showing the coach's capacity.**

*Chapter Two*

# 1915 – Deepening Conflict

A young lieutenant, serving with the Gloucestershire Regiment, wrote to his mother in early January about his Christmas in the trenches. The letter read:

> *I spent a happy Christmas Day on neutral ground situated between our trenches and the Germans (only 200 yards away) singing Christmas carols to the German soldiers. My platoon joined in the chorus, much to the amusement of the Germans.*

On 14 January, a Gloucester corporal, in the 2nd Gloucester Regiment, wrote home from the Front:

**Tom Wiltshire with members of the 1/6th Battalion of the Gloucestershire Regiment.**

**The first church parade in connection with the Badgeworth and District Men's and Women's Voluntary Aid Detachments of the British Red Cross Society took place on the afternoon of Sunday, 10 January 1915. The men, complete with their commandant, Dr Moore, paraded seventy-strong at the Cross Roads, while the ladies assembled at Badgeworth Court.**

*We have had our first experience of trench life. It is a case of 'get out and get under' here, with bullets zipping around one. Going to and from the trenches, the German snipers won't even let you alone.*

*It is lovely standing in water, mud and slush, knee-deep, and lying in dug-outs for hours suffering with cold. I did not know I had a pair of feet until I*

**The Red Cross Society, the Badgeworth Voluntary Aid Detachments, at their first church parade on Saturday, 10 January 1915. The photo shows Quarter-Master C.A. Crane (The Reddings), Lady Cunynghame (Commandant of Ladies' Section) and her son, Dr R.D.M. Moore (Commandant of Men's Section).**

**A silk postcard from 1915. These were bought in France and sent back to loved ones in Great Britain.**

*touched them. Even yet, many of our men do not realise they are at war; they are happy enough as long as their feet keep warm and cigarette between their lips. Our men were in the trenches for 48 hours; the casualties were about five, including two hit by snipers. Our machine gunners are perfectly well. I consider I am lucky to be alive now. We are the luckiest regiment so far, with none killed.*

On Sunday, 17 January, a concert was arranged at the Palladium in aid of the Belgian Refugee Relief Fund. At the concert, Mrs George Bland sang *Love is meant to make us glad* and *The little road home*. Mr Yorke Bailey contributed *A song of Thanksgiving* and *I hear you calling me*, which were both well-received.

On Tuesday, 19 January, a party of ten soldiers, suffering from either frostbite or wounds, arrived in Gloucester from Bristol at 6.00 pm. Nine of the cases needed stretchers while the other case was driven to the Red Cross Hospital by car. Messrs Blinkhorn and Son lent one of their vans so that the stretchers could be accommodated. A cello solo, *Romance sans paroles,* was played by Miss A. Fluck while Mr Ernest Fane, an elocutionist, recited *Devil may care*. Many other acts took part and the concert was a great success.

During January, a party of schoolboys, residing in the Kingsholm district, arranged a series of small concerts to raise funds to supply twelve mouth organs to soldiers serving at the Front. As a result of the entertainment already performed, three mouth organs had been sent to the Front and Master M. Lees of Kings House, Gloucester, received an acknowledgement from Gunner A.J. Tranter, of the 17th Battery RFA, 2nd Division, who wrote:

> *I am taking the opportunity on behalf of my chums, to thank you very much indeed for the generous manner in which you filled up the gap in our little bivouac. We are now able to have quite a lively evening after a somewhat tedious time surrounded by water and mud. I have also written to thank the editor of the* Daily Mirror *for his kindness in forwarding your gift to us. Once we came upon an old Belgian melodeon in a deserted farmhouse but the arrangement of the notes differed so much from the English that we had, in the finish, to bid it 'Good-bye!'*

Towards the end of January, it was announced that the subscriptions to the Mayor of Gloucester's Fund for the provision of Christmas gifts for soldiers and sailors totalled £122 6s 10d. Generous supplies of plum puddings and other gifts were also received, which the railway company happily carried free of charge. A total of £101 9s 2d was spent on jerseys, socks, khaki helmets and mittens. An additional £25 5s was spent on plum puddings, soap, tea and newspapers, etc. Other expenses incurred including railway costs for an official to travel with the gifts. Printing and postage meant there was a deficit of £7 9s, and the mayor appealed for further donations to cover these costs.

At the beginning of February, Mrs G. Barnes received a postcard from her husband, Private Barnes, of the 1st Gloucestershire Regiment, saying that he was a prisoner-of-war at Doeberitz. His note said he was in the best of health and had recovered well from his wounds. He acknowledged receipt of 10s and asked for tobacco, cigarettes and money, if it could be spared, as he was in great need of it.

Driver D. Snowden, of the 94th RFA, wrote to his mother, Mrs J.C. Snowden of 55 Widden Street, Gloucester, saying:

> *We are having a rotten time of it with the weather and to make it worse, we get shelled every day. But we take little notice of them*

**An advert in the *Gloucester Journal* of Saturday, 23 January 1915, appealing for 300 recruits for the Royal Field Artillery (1st Reserve) Brigade. Men were required to be at least 5 feet 3 inches in height and to be over 18 years and 9 months.**

*now. Our chaps laugh like blazes when any shells come over; they shout 'H.L.I.' nearly every time. But you should see them nip when one bursts above their heads. You should also see the expressions on the faces of some of the draft we have just had from home; it's the first time they have been under shell fire. People at home think it's a picnic or a time of pleasure but some of them ought to come out here and see and perhaps they would realise something of it.*

"LEND A HAND."

Play a Man's part, and enlist to-day.
You will learn the address of the nearest Recruiting Office at any Post Office.

**A cartoon, which appeared in the *Gloucester Journal* of Saturday 23 January 1915, encouraging men to enlist in the army and 'do their bit'.**

On Wednesday, 24 February, a route march took place between Cheltenham and Gloucester. The 10th Battalion of the Gloucester Regiment, comprising 500 men and under the command of Lieutenant Colonel Pritchard, left their headquarters at about 9.45 am and proceeded to Coombe Hill and then

**A view of Northgate Street showing a busy scene complete with horses and carts and a tram.**

on to Gloucester. It became common knowledge that they would be arriving in the city about 2 hours earlier. A huge crowd formed on the London Road shortly before 12 o'clock. However, the troops arrived half-an-hour later and entered the city by way of Worcester Street and proceeded via Northgate Street, Westgate Street and College Street to College Green. After being dismissed, they had lunch. After refreshments, the soldiers returned to Cheltenham by the main route. Their visit had caused great excitement and their procession through the streets was witnessed by large crowds.

The *Gloucester Journal* of 27 February reported that Private George Cook, of the Gloucester Regiment, hadn't been killed as reported three months earlier. Cook, a well-known Oldham and Gloucester three-quarter, was discovered wounded but well and a prisoner of the Germans. News of his untimely death had come from a comrade in a letter to Cook's parents, Mr and Mrs J. Cook of 84 Alvin Street. On Monday, 15 February, the War Office confirmed his death but the information later proved to be incorrect.

Mr and Mrs Cook, however, later received a postcard from their son, stating that he was a prisoner-of-war in a hospital at Lille but was doing well. The first indication that Private Cook was still alive and well came via a soldier from a member of the London Scottish Regiment, who had promised to contact Cook's parents on returning to Great Britain. The soldier had been in hospital with Private Cook but was allowed to return home under a scheme that allowed the exchange of disabled prisoners. It was reported that Private Cook had sustained a gunshot wound to the back, but was being cared for by a French doctor and nurse who had been taken prisoner at the same time.

**Private George Cook, a former Oldham and Gloucester three-quarter, had been reported killed in a letter sent home by a friend. However, it was later discovered that Cook was alive and well when his parents received a postcard from a comrade stating he was a prisoner at Lille, where he was in hospital being treated for a gunshot wound to the back. The story appeared in the *Gloucester Journal* of Saturday, 27 February 1915.**

Towards the end of February, Mr J.B. Minahan wrote to the local paper saying that he had visited Private J.G. Halford, formerly the captain of the Gloucester Football Club, in hospital and that 'he is happy and doing well'.

On Monday, 8 March, at a meeting at the Guildhall, Colonel Sir Arthur Anstice announced that another 1,000 men were required from Gloucester for the army.

**Members of the Gloucester Regiment at camp in Little Baddow, Essex, on 31 March 1915 just prior to embarkation to France.**

The *Cheltenham Chronicle* noted:

*This is a somewhat large order and without in any way wishing to disparage the good efforts of those engaged in obtaining the necessary number of men to assist in the bringing about of the end of the great war, one cannot help thinking that it will be a difficult*

**The Army Service Corps performing as a rag-time band, at a Voluntary Aid Hospital, in March 1915. Included in the photo is Private Ray of the 2nd Gloucesters.**

**Unloading horses from a ship at Gallipoli in 1915. Horses played a vital role in the war effort, especially in conflicts such as the Gallipoli Campaign. The campaign was fought to secure a sea route to Russia, with the British and French launching a naval offensive, forcing a passage through the Dardanelles. The ensuing land battle failed with the loss of many lives, including many Australians and New Zealanders.**

*task indeed to raise another thousand men from the old city. The Mayor, who has done so much for recruiting and also for recruits, took the opportunity of once more impressing on the War Office, through Colonel Gretton (Assistant Inspector of Recruiting of the Southern Command), his firm belief that if another battalion was stationed in our midst it would be a great inducement to men to join the colours. His Worship pointed out the many advantages possessed by Gloucester for the billeting and training of men and also once more suggested the provision of badges for those who had offered their services but had been refused as medically unfit. Colonel Gretton assured the Mayor that his suggestions should be brought before the proper authorities who, he said, fully recognised the excellent response to the call of arms by Gloucester men.*

Lord Bathurst suggested at the meeting that some form of compulsory enlistment should be introduced, but this suggestion wasn't favourably received by some members of the audience. They were also unhappy about his reference to engineers who refused to work for more than eight hours a day. Mr Abel Evans stated that had conscription been in place at the present time, then much more hardship would have been felt by the city owing to men of eligible age being taken away from large factories such at the Wagon Works and Messrs Fielding and Platt. He pointed out that a great quantity of goods for the War Office and the navy were being turned out from the two factories on a daily basis.

At a meeting of the Board of Governors in Gloucester in March, it was stated that war was playing havoc in the homes of the poor. Mr E.P. Little suggested that there should be an advance of an additional 3d

Private C. Ireland died of wounds sustained in the fighting at Le Bassée. He had served seven years with the 1st Battalion Gloucestershire Regiment, of which five years were spent with the Colours in India. He joined the reserve in November 1911 and subsequently was employed as a porter at Gloucester Great Western Railway Station, from where he was called-up to join his old regiment on the outbreak of war.

Corporal George T. Phillips was killed on 25 February 1915 while serving with the 2nd Gloucester Regiment. His captain wrote back to his parents: 'He was shot through the head and killed instantly while in the trenches during a hot burst of fire with the enemy. He was buried immediately behind the trench and I put a strong wooden cross on his grave. I can only say he was a very great friend of mine and you have my deepest sympathy.'

to enable families to cope with the increasing cost of coal. Mr Gwynne Evans stated that the cost of living had advanced by 5s in the pound. However, Mr J.C.C. Cummins, in charge of finances, struck a warning note, saying that while he realised that the cost of living had risen dramatically, each hardship case should be considered on its own basis and there shouldn't be an 'across the board' rise for everyone.

On 10 April, Gunner Arthur Taylor, the son of Walter Taylor who formerly played football for Gloucester, wrote home from 'Somewhere in Belgium':

*We are in action but are all safe and well. Don't worry over me, for where we are is nearly as safe as Broomfield.*

On Thursday, 15 April, the Drum and Fife Band of the 2/5th Gloucesters, together with a recruiting party, left Gloucester by train in the morning en route to Wickwar. After dinner they marched to Hawkesbury Upton, where they billeted for the night.

On Saturday, 17 April, the *Gloucester Journal* carried a story under the headline 'Gifts from the Match Factory'. It read:

*There has been dispatched to the front, to the 1st Gloucesters and others, a further £2 12s worth of tobacco and cigarettes from the tobacco fund of Messrs Moreland's Match Works employees and staff.*

*The Officer commanding the 2nd Gloucesters has written*

**Tom Wiltshire at camp with members of the Gloucester Regiment.**

**Non-commissioned officers of the Cyclist Company in April 1915.**

*acknowledging, with sincere thanks, gifts of a case of matches and a parcel of tobacco and cigarettes sent by the employees of Messrs S.J. Moreland and Sons Ltd. Referring to the matches, the commander says:* 'T.A. is always happy if he has his own box of lights.'

On Monday, 19 April at noon, there was a march through the city by the Yeomanry, Cyclists' Corps and Scouts. The Gloucester Civil Training Corps and the British Boy and Baden Powell Scouts also paraded through the principal streets of the city on Saturdays and on Monday evenings.

During April, Gunner W. Plenning, of the Gloucester Royal Field Artillery, wrote to his mother at 37 Seymour Road, Gloucester. His letter read:

*I am now in the fighting line and in a pleased mood. I find that the dug-outs are*

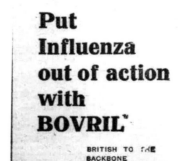

An advert stating: 'Put influenza out of action with Bovril. British to the backbone.' The advert appeared in the *Gloucester Journal* during March 1915.

**The 11th Section, A Company of the 1/6th Gloucesters posing for a regimental photo.**

During April 1915, the Drum and Fife Band of the 2/5th Gloucesters, together with a recruiting party, completed a tour of Stroud and other districts before returning to the Drill Hall at Brunswick Road, Gloucester. Over seventy new recruits enlisted for the 3rd line battalion of the 5th Gloucesters and thirty men enlisted in other regiments.

*really comfortable affairs, with board floors, shelves and fire places, and even doors in some cases. We have named our shanty 'The Monks Retreat', in remembrance of dear old Gloucester, and we have a chap here who is an expert in the art of modelling and he is decorating the place with models made of clay. Behind us lies a ruined little township. It was once prosperous, I think, but now it bears testimony to the Germans' big guns. Of course, the church was shelled and it is most noticable that the greatest damage has been done around the church, around which lie great 'J.J.' holes. Our battery has shelled the German positions here, so you see we have been in action. This morning, a shell burst when I was washing our mess tins and it made quite a rotten row, but it was nowhere near me.*

The *Gloucester Journal* of Saturday, 8 May carried the story of recruitment within the police force of Gloucester. It read:

*The great value of a concerted recruiting movement, such as that which has been conducted in the ranks of the Gloucestershire Constabulary, is that the men enlisting are able to make common choice of the Army unit in which they will serve and the heavy battery which the Gloucester constables have joined will be almost exclusively a police unit and, therefore, a 'pals company' in the fullest sense of the word. The Gloucester and Bristol police have together formed two such batteries and having regard to the quality of recruits and the perfection of drill and discipline to which they had attained in the police force, they should rapidly qualify for the Front. Certainly if it should be their fortune to engage in active operations on the Western battle front or elsewhere, the men may be relied upon to render a good account of themselves. Perhaps it was natural enough, that at Wednesday's complimentary proceedings, an optimistic tone should have prevailed. No one could have looked upon so fine a body of men without feeling a greater degree of confidence in the ability of the country to uphold its just cause. Of course, it has to be recognised that they are far above the average standard of recruit obtainable at any period of the war; but it is men of this stamp who stiffen any unit to which they become attached and happily England has not by any means exhausted her supply of such and their splendid enthusiasm in offering their services cannot but be heartening to all who are concerned, whether in the fighting line at the Front or in the mobilisation and organisation of our resources at home in upholding the country's honour and obligations.*

*Unfortunately, the pleasure of the send-off which has been given to the Gloucester police recruits is tinged with regret that the County Authority is debarred, under the limitations of the Police Acts, from treating them with the same generosity as other classes of county employees who have similarly offered their services. The concessions submitted to parliament are satisfactory, as far as they go, in securing to these soldier policemen the full advantages of the police pensions scheme but they do not allow the police authority to supplement military pay. The fact that 25 percent of the force have been perfectly ready to make large financial sacrifices in order to meet the country's supreme need redounds all the more to their credit.*

An advert for D. Lane and Sons which appeared in the *Gloucester Journal* on 1 May 1915. The company supplied made-to-measure service boots and leggings for serving officers.

During May, the annual review and official cadet inspection of the 1st Gloucester Diocesan Battalion of the Church Lads' Brigade was held at Gloucester on Whit Monday, which coincided with Empire Day. The inspection was carried out by Colonel Sir Arthur Anstice KCB, chairman of the Gloucestershire Territorial Association.

The proceedings commenced at 11.15 am, when the battalion assembled at the cattle market and headed off fifteen minutes later accompanied by a massed bugle band, travelling via Clarence Street, Eastgate Street and Westgate Street and on to the cathedral. A special service was held by the Reverend Canon Ridsdale. At 5.00 pm, the officers and lads were entertained to tea at the Northgate Mansions by the officers and friends of the All Saint's Company, Gloucester.

On 21 May, a meeting of the Gloucestershire War Relief Committee was held at the Shire Hall to consider an application from the County Voluntary Aid (Red Cross) Society for a grant of £1,000. The money was needed for equipment for local hospitals, which altogether housed 500 patients.

The New Gloucester Red Cross Hospital, Voluntary Aid Detachment No. 96 at Hillfield. The caption to the photo, in the *Gloucester Journal* of Saturday, 12 June 1915, read: 'This photograph is of the Red Cross Voluntary Aid Detachment Glos. 96, taken on the Terrace of Hillfield, which has been prepared as a Voluntary Aid Hospital by the members of the detachment, and is now standing absolutely ready for occupation. The medical officer in charge is Dr Dykes Bower and the Lady Superintendent, Mrs Courteau.'

Women and war work. The Berkeley Agricultural Society's milking competition showing a section of women and girl competitors, 12 June 1915.

On Sunday, 20 June, the Gloucester Volunteer Training Corps held a drum-head service on the Spa cricket field. A large crowd gathered and they were joined by the mayor and mayoress, the city high sheriff as well as a number of wounded men from the Great Western Road Red Cross Hospital. The corps, under the command of Mr H.G. Norman, was headed by a bugle band and marched their way from Kingsholm to the Spa, where they formed in a square. The Reverend Cecil Williams said prayers and the lesson were read by the city high sheriff. The Wagon Works Silver Band accompanied the hymns, which included *All people that on earth do dwell, Eternal Father strong to save* and *God, the all terrible* (the Russian National Anthem). The lord bishop of the diocese gave an address, saying that there were two kinds of courage, physical courage and spiritual courage. The service ended with a verse of the National Anthem.

**Lance Corporal E. Keveren was killed on 9 May 1915. He was an army reservist and previously worked for the M.R. Goods Department in Gloucester. On signing up, he was attached to the 1st Gloucester Regiment. He was one of seven soldier sons of Mrs Keverne of Seymour Road, Gloucester, and left a wife and small child.**

On Monday, 21 June, a concert was held at Coombe Hill in aid of the Red Cross. Over 200 people attended the event, which included songs, violin-playing, piano and banjo duets as well as humorous recitals. Many people called for encores but these weren't always granted due to the length of the programme. As a result of the concert, the Boddington Red Cross Hospital received a substantial addition to its funds.

An article appeared in the *Cheltenham Chronicle* of Saturday, 26 June. Under the headline 'Gloucester Women and the War', it read:

*Although there are on the war service register of the Gloucester*

**An advert for Reynolds' Wheatmeal Bread, which appeared in the *Gloucester Journal* of Saturday, 29 May 1915. The advert stated that British soldiers inprisoned in Germany had specifically requested the bread.**

While on his way from Bristol to Malvern in June 1915, David Lloyd George spent an hour with the Dean of Gloucester. The minister of munitions had hoped to spend a quiet hour at the cathedral, but his chauffeur had had to ask directions, and Lloyd George was recognised. Within a few minutes, a large crowd of admirers had gathered at College Green. The tremendous welcome included cheer after cheer, and there was much appreciation of Lloyd George's contribution to the war.

*Labour Exchange the names of a large number of women who have expressed their willingness to undertake various forms of employment in order to release young men for military duties, employers in and around the city have, so far, been slow to avail themselves to the opportunities thus afforded for them securing female labour. The exchange has been instrumental in supplying a great many women for fruit picking and packing. Women are being employed as railway*

A photo showing the 6th Gloucesters in training. They were formed at St Michael's Hill, Bristol, in September 1914 as part of a home service unit. Most men shown hadn't yet been issued with uniforms, although some had their own rifles.

*carriage cleaners and vacancies in banks have been filled by young ladies.*

During June, Private Claude G. Bullingham, of the 1/5th Gloucesters, wrote home to his mother from a 'dug-out somewhere in France'. He wrote that he was as happy as a sandboy and as fit as a fiddle, and that a kindly sergeant had given him a haircut. He said that they had the luxury of hot baths, a change of underclothes and a steaming of suits when the men left the trenches for their barn. He continued:

*We enjoy ourselves out here. We have quite a little holiday when we are on our rest and can draw money (French, of course) every time we go out of the trench. When we are on rest in the barns, we have a proper flare up. We can buy a bit extra and we have some good old songs. With the mouth-organ, tin whistle and a biscuit tin, we have got a good band and we don't half make a din. You can hear us a long way before you get to us. They keep on with it and there are plenty to sing in turns and we join in the 'coal-box.' I give them a 'rouster' now and then. Yes, we enjoy ourselves out here alright and are all happy.*

An advert appeared in the *Gloucester Journal* of 19 July appealing for recruits for the Gloucestershire Royal Field Artillery (3rd line).

**Members of the Gloucestershire Regiment in Italy in 1918.**

Minimum height required was 5 feet 3 inches and the minimum age was 19. Vacancies also existed for saddlers, farriers, shoeing smiths and wheelwrights, and anyone interested was asked to apply to Warrant Officer Conway Jones, Northgate, Gloucester.

A report in the *Western Times* of 26 July told of Gloucester Wagon Works and the war. The article read:

*Mr R.V. Vassar-Smith (chairman of the Gloucester Railway Carriage and Wagon Company) on Saturday afternoon opened the annual fruit, flower and vegetable show in connection with the undertaking. In doing so, he said that 902 men engaged at the works volunteered for services with the colours, of which number 779 were actually serving and 123 were, for various reasons, not taken. Although this percentage of men was greater than any he knew of in any other place, it would be still greater if those who were detained at the works were not forced to be there by reason of the work they were doing for the government for war purposes. Therefore every man at the works was doing his share in helping those who were gone out to the front and in that way was serving his country. It appeared that 33 members of the works ambulance corps were now in army service. Mr Vassar-Smith asked Mr Alfred Brown's acceptance of a medal and a cheque for £5 from the directors as recognition of long and faithful service, he having been uninterruptedly at the works for a period of 50 years.*

The *Gloucester Journal* of Saturday, 28 August, reported that Lance Corporal Edgar Taylor, of Moor Street, was still a prisoner in Germany. In an earlier article, he had requested that his mother send him a tin of treacle to help the month-old bread they were given 'to go down'. Afterwards, he asked for some bread to be sent out, which he received and described as 'beautiful!' and asked for more.

Entertainment continued in the city and the *Gloucester Journal* reported on the week's entertainment at the Hippodrome towards the end of August. The article read:

*For a second time within a few weeks, the*

Sergeant A.E. Hatton, aged 34, of Wellesley Street, Gloucester, was killed on 28 July 1915, 'somewhere in France'. Hatton had been employed by the Gloucester County Council for ten years and had been a reservist who was recalled to the colours on 5 August 1914. He left a widow and one child.

*Hippodrome has secured star turns of first magnitude. This week, the chief attraction is George Lashwood. It is no misnomer to call him the Beau Brummell of the vaudeville stage and one can understand that his dicta in matters of stage etiquette are as indisputable as ever were those pronounced by the original Beau Brummell in a wider sphere a hundred years ago. He had a good reception and contributed four songs 'I'm on the jury' (brewery) – by the way, have we not outgrown this bibulous song? – 'I've got to do my duty,' another about a shy couple and 'Where are the lads of the village tonight?' which is his latest success.*

*Miss Edith Fink, who is a dainty comedienne, also gives two songs, 'Johnny with the new clothes on' and another descriptive of an ill-assorted couple, both of which immediately caught on. Another musical item is the performance on two xylophones by Miss Rosie Roy, which is a marvel of dexterity and skill. One of the drollest and cleverest turns is Ted Mercel, comedian and acrobatic skate dancer.*

**Driver R.G. Crockett was badly wounded on 9 May 1915 after being struck in both legs, back, shoulder and head. He was also poisoned by gas. He recovered from his wounds and joined the 2/3rd Regiment in readiness for further service.**

Second Lieutenant Jack Stone wrote to the *Gloucester Journal* late in August with a request. It read:

*On behalf of the men of the 3/6th Gloucesters now in camp, I am appealing to your readers for any old or new boxing gloves, footballs or cricket bats, also socks, all of which are urgently needed.*

On Wednesday, 8 September, a soldier appeared at the Gloucester police court charged with deception. The local newspapers reported the case:

*At Gloucester police court on Wednesday, Daniel Reed, a private in the 13th Gloucesters, was charged with obtaining food and lodgings, to the extent of 7s and 6d, by false pretences, from Annie Elizabeth Bowstill, of Bearland House, Longsmith Street, between Aug. 25 and 28.*

*Prosecutrix, the wife of Ernest Arthur Bowskill, a soldier, stated that while in Westgate Street on Aug. 25, she saw prisoner walking*

Private W.J. Parker of A Company, 7th Gloucesters, who was killed in action at Gallipoli on 26 July 1915. He was the son of Mr W. N. Parker, Citizen' Office Tewkesbury.

Sergeant W.H.L. Hawkes of the Royal Berkshire Regiment was killed in action on 28 August 1915. His parents were Mr and Mrs Hawkes of Newton Street, Coney Hill, Gloucester. Sergeant Hawkes had previously worked at Reynold's Flour Mill.

Private Howard Selwyn of Minsterworth, who died of wounds received in the Dardanelles. Private Selwyn died on 10 August 1915 while fighting at Gallipoli. He was 25 years old and had formerly been employed at the Wagon Works in Gloucester.

Private J. Westwood of the 8th Welsh Regiment, who was wounded in action in the Dardanelles on 8 August 1915. Private Westwood was the son of Mr and Mrs Westwood of 98 Alma Place, Gloucester.

*along with a stick. She asked him what was the matter and he replied that he had been through the war and was wounded and had been in hospital for seven months. Witness enquired if his home was in Gloucester and he replied that he had not a friend in the world. He added that he had been at a lodging house and*

George Morgan of 13 Regent Street, Gloucester, of the Royal Naval Reserve, who was wounded in action while on board RMS *Andania*. The news was reported in the *Gloucester Journal* of Saturday, 4 September 1915. Morgan was admitted to the Royal Naval Hospital, Plymouth, suffering from shrapnel wounds to the chest, back and right arm. He was formerly a Gloucester fireman and a diver at the docks. He had served on two ships, the *Ocean* and *Triumph*, which were sunk by the enemy, but he escaped with little more than a 'ducking'.

**An advert for Bird's Spongie, featured in the Gloucester Journal of 11 September 1915, suggested you 'make at home tasty and dainty Swiss Roll more than equal to the finest shop roll'.**

*could get no rest as there were four other men in the room, remarking that he paid 1s 6d a night. He also stated that £10 mobilisation money and £7 arrears of pay was due to him from the military authorities. Witness agreed to board and lodge him and told him she would be a good friend to him if he would be straight. He stayed three nights. He said that he would see her right when he received his mobilisation money.*

*Sergt. Godding, of the 13th Gloucesters, formerly a Gloucester police constable, said on Aug. 29 he saw prisoner sitting on a doorstep in St. Aldate Street, saluting passersby. He enquired 'Well, Reed, what's the game?' and Reed replied that he was going to rejoin his regiment. Witness told him that he intended to hand him over to the police and prisoner said he would give him £2 if he let him go. Witness took him to the police station and on the way, prisoner bolted and witness overtook him. Red had never been to the front and had been absent without leave since Aug. 22. Prisoner was not entitled to any money but was really indebted to his regiment owing to misconduct. Prisoner stated that the trouble was caused through his wife living with another man. He had money in the post office. Prisoner had previously been convicted of similar offences.*

In sentencing prisoner to three months' imprisonment with hard labour, the chairman (Mr. H.G. Robinson) characterised it as a particularly heartless fraud.

In the *Gloucester Journal* of Saturday, 16 October, a letter from a Gloucester private in the

**A popular collector for the Prince of Wales' Fund, named as Mrs Firmin Cuthbert's dog, 'Dice', appeared in the *Gloucester Journal* of Saturday, 19 September 1914.**

10th Gloucesters told of life in the trenches. It read:

> We are still in the trenches, where we have been since last Tuesday night. How long we are in for I cannot say. We get no rest whatsoever. On Friday afternoon, the Germans counter-attacked and were repulsed. There was terrible gun-fire on each side for four hours, which was a very trying time. It was hell on earth when the artillery was on with its terrible destruction; French, English and German guns were all going off together. The Germans are trying desperately hard to regain their lost trenches but cannot do so. We were waiting for them on Friday when their infantry made a poor attack and were soon repulsed.

King George V became king on 6 May 1910. The German kaiser, Wilhelm II, was the king's first cousin. Many of the royal family had German titles due to their descent. George changed the name of the British royal house on 17 July 1917 from the House of Saxe-Coburg and Gotha to the House of Windsor. The former name was felt to be too German-sounding for the British public. Both he and his relatives relinquished all their German titles soon after.

Meanwhile, during October, several recruits wrote to the local paper from France stating that they had been enjoying playing games of rugby football during the few days rest they had from the trenches. Men of the 1/5th Gloucesters took part and one match took place between C and D companies. Men said that the weather was splendid and the match attracted a huge crowd of Tommies. A French gentleman consented to kick-off and both teams were described as 'exceptionally keen' and the play was fast. The game was won by D Company with the end result being 6 tries to nil.

As winter set in in Northern Europe, appeals for woollens for the troops appeared in local newspapers. One letter, in the *Gloucester Journal* of Saturday, 30 October read:

An advert for a free cookery demonstration arranged by Brown and Polson during October 1915. The event was held at the Glevum Hall, Southgate, Gloucester.

**Great interest was displayed at the railway station, on the afternoon of 21 October 1914, when a hospital train arrived containing wounded Belgian soldiers. The men were not very seriously wounded and most walked from the station to the hospital.**

*Woollen Helmets.*

*Dear Sir, I am endeavouring to collect by November 10th (or sooner if possible) 100-130 woollen helmets for the men of C Battery, 49th Brigade R.F.A., now 'somewhere in France.' Your readers have in the past been very generous in answering appeals. May I trespass upon their bounty yet again and ask them to help me to send at least the hundred helmets asked for? The nights are very cold now and the helmets would be a great comfort to the men. I should be glad to give knitting directions or answer any questions if anyone would like to write to me.*

*Yours truly,*

*Blanche Ancrum.*
*14 Barton Street, Gloucester.*

A further letter was published in the same edition from the Mayoress of Gloucester, which read:

**Richard Thomas Guest, an engine room artificer, was reported killed when HMS *Hawke* was sunk by a German submarine on 15 October 1914. He was well-known in Gloucester and had previously won a scholarship at Widden Street Council School, which admitted him to Sir Thomas Rich's School. When he was 16, he passed the exam in London to become a boy artificer and was the first boy from the school to obtain this honour.**

*The Mayoress's Appeal.*

*Dear Sir, Will you allow me through the medium of your paper to thank all those kind friends who so generously subscribed to my appeal for Furber's Hand Ambulances; especially the Rev. Canon Park, of Highnam Vicarage, for his generous gift of an ambulance, fully equipped, in memory of his mother. This enabled me to send two to the front, one to the 1st Gloucesters and one to the 3rd Gloucesters. I have some money towards a third and I'm very anxious to send two more. Any donations, however small, will be greatly acknowledged by me.*

Yours sincerely,

Rosa Bruton.

(Mayoress of Gloucester).

On the afternoon of Sunday, 7 November, there was a large muster of the Gloucester Volunteer Training Corps who followed a two-hour route-march through the city. It gave many people their first chance to inspect the troops at close hand in the resplendence of their new uniforms. On returning to headquarters, Commander H.G. Norman expressed to the corps his gratitude for rallying around him during his time as recruitment officer. He stated that an advert placed in *The Citizen* over three nights for recruits received no more than a dozen applicants. He said that he felt that 'there were plenty gentlemen of leisure and influence who might have undertaken this duty in response to the Mayor's appeal and thus spared the members of the Corps the march who were doing excellent service elsewhere'.

He said the failure of people to come forward placed the recruiting committee in great difficulty, there was a great necessity for canvassing to take place without delay and he knew that he could rely on the loyalty and co-operation of members of the corps.

Russian Flag Day was held in Gloucester on 20 November and a total of £107 16s 10d was collected. The mayoress received a letter from the honorary secretary dealing with the collection, which read:

*May I, on behalf of the Executive Committee, ask you to accept for yourself, and express to your workers, our sincere thanks for all they have done and for the splendid result of their efforts. We think*

**Private Albert Hemmings, a reservist in the Gloucester Regiment, was killed in action during the First Battle of the Aisne on 26 September 1914. He was the brother of Mr W. Hemmings of 51 Granville Street, Gloucester, and was well-known both in the city and in Stroud.**

Comforts for the navy on HMS *Gloucester*. 'Bounce' is shown wearing one of the scarves sent by a Gloucester lady for the men of HMS *Gloucester,* as featured in the *Gloucester Journal* of Saturday, 21 November 1914.

A competition appeared in the *Gloucester Journal* of Saturday, 21 November 1914. Nestlé's Milk offered prizes worth over £5,600. Entrants were asked to estimate the number of tins of Nestlé's Milk and Milkmaid Milk sold during a twelve-month period. Prizes ranged from 5 shillings to £200, as well as 500 boxes of Nestlé's milk chocolates.

*Gloucester has responded magnificently and we are more than grateful for all the trouble you have taken and for the success achieved. Only yesterday, we received a telegram from her Imperial Majesty the Czarina laying stress on the value of our work and explaining that the assistance she is receiving from our Fund goes to purchase medical comforts for the wounded which are sent to the front in special Red Cross trains.*

A letter appeared in the *Gloucester Journal* of Saturday, 4 December, which featured an appeal from the mayor. It read:

*Last year, I made an appeal through the local press and was enabled to forward plum puddings and other Christmas gifts, such as warm gloves, mufflers, socks, mittens, pipes, chocolates etc., to the officers and men of H.M.S. Gloucester and of the 1st Battalion of the Gloucestershire Regiment.*

*Another Christmas will soon be here and I think many of the inhabitants of the city and neighbourhood of Gloucester would desire that some kindly greeting and token of Christmas should be sent to the officers and men of H.M.S. Gloucester and of the Gloucestershire Regiments now serving abroad, so far as that may be practicable. I shall, therefore, be glad to receive plum puddings or other Christmas gifts or subscriptions which will enable me to provide them.*

*Plum puddings, which may be of different sizes, say 1, 2 or 4 lbs., must not be sent in basins but should be wrapped in greaseproof or parchment paper and securely packed in boxes or parcels on which the contents should be clearly marked. Any of the gifts may have a note or card attached giving the name and address of the sender and a suitable Christmas greeting.*

*Subscriptions and gifts should be marked 'Christmas Gifts for Sailors and Soldiers' and sent to me at the Guildhall on or before the 10th December.*

Instructions were sent to relatives of those fighting telling them what to include in Christmas parcels sent to the Front. They were told not to send perishables, bottles, pudding basins, etc., which were all prohibited. From 1 December, the maximum weight of a parcel was reduced to 7lb and all parcels had to be packed in covers of canvas, linen or other strong material. The name and address of the sender had to be written on the outside, otherwise the parcel might not be delivered. Christmas Day letters were to be posted no later than 17 December, and parcels were to be posted before 13 December.

The Gloucester Great Christmas Market was held on 13 December. It included the sale of: *'385 grand fat bullocks, heifers and cows; 750 choice fat sheep; 700 bacon pigs, porkers and heavy sows as well as 80 calves.'*

The *Gloucester Journal* of 18 December requested playing cards for troops stationed locally. The story read:

*Lance-Corpl. W. S. Cull asks for the loan of gift of a few packs of playing cards for the use of men of the 3/1st R.G.H.Y., stationed at Longford House near Gloucester during the Christmas holidays, when a whist drive has been arranged. Every effort is being made to make the men as comfortable and happy as possible for Christmas and any help in this direction would be much appreciated. The receipt of any other indoor games would, of course, be very acceptable.*

On 25 December, the Palace Theatre announced its entertainment for Christmas, which included Leon Vint and Jack Mackenzie's *Panto Vue* and *Pretty Darlings*. It was described as: *'a gorgeous mixture of pantomime and up-to-date revue including Gloucester's own comedian, Jack Mackenzie and his delightfully delicious delectable dainty damsels. Real Bon Bouches. New scenery, dresses and appointments.'*

**Meals in the trenches usually consisted of bully, beef but behind the lines, the food could be quite varied, as shown here on Christmas Day 1915. A tray of plump chickens has been prepared for the men as they are called to the cookhouse by a bugler of the Army Veterinary Corps.**

*Chapter Three*

# 1916 – The Realization

The *Gloucester Journal* of 1 January reported that in spite of the war, inmates of the workhouse voted the previous Christmas celebrations 'as good as ever'. Christmas gifts were received from the mayor and mayoress and included crackers, oranges and one shilling each for the fourteen children staying there. The city high sheriff gave sweets and tobacco, Sir Hubert Parry gave a Christmas tree and evergreens, Captain J.D. Birchall and Mrs Siveter also gave evergreens, and Mr A.E. Bretherton and Mrs L.E. Garnham gave money to provide the old women at Ladybelegate Lodge with tea. Other gifts included a basket of pears, jam, sauce and pickles and the loan of flags for the infirmary ward.

The newspaper reported:

*As usual, the celebrations commenced with a service in the chapel, the preacher being the Chaplain (the Rev. C. Davis). When the dinner bell sounded, the inmates trooped into their gaily-decorated dining rooms to partake of an abundant feast of roast beef, baked and boiled potatoes, parsnips and Brussels sprouts, plum pudding, with plenty of beer or lemonade to complete the meal. The sick and the women were*

A recruitment poster stating: 'Women of Britain say "Go!" In January 1916 the Military Service Bill was introduced, forcing the conscription of single men between the ages of 18 and 41. In May, conscription was extended to married men also.

*provided with jam tarts and oranges, whilst the men received gifts of tobacco and the non-smokers a supply of sugar and tea. The children enjoyed biscuits and sweets. The children, after dinner, were provided with a Christmas tree. This was erected in the day room and presented a pretty appearance being loaded with crackers and toys.*

**The 4th Reserve Battalion of the Gloucestershire Regiment, gathered at Cheltenham in 1916.**

In the New Year's Honours list, the Mayor of Gloucester, Councillor James Bruton, received a knighthood, much to the delight of the people of Gloucester.

On 8 January, a meeting was held at the Shire Hall of the Gloucestershire War Agricultural Committee where the chairman, Mr M.W. Colchester-Wemyss, read a letter from the Board of Agriculture regarding the export of produce to foreign countries. It was stated that it was the policy of the board to allow produce to be exported to neutral countries, although in limited quantities that wouldn't be detrimental to British farmers.

The chairman mentioned a question raised at a previous meeting, which asked if schoolgirls would be allowed to stay at home so that their mothers were able to work on the land. The Education Committee had responded, saying that they were anxious to assist farmers and, if they were satisfied that there was a demand for mothers to work on the land, they would consider each case on its merits.

Mr F. Baber asked if boys of 12 years and older would be allowed to work on the land. Mr F.A. Hyett replied that they would be able to work on the land as long as the Education Committee was happy that all efforts had been made to obtain ordinary labourers.

Mr H. W. Househald, the secretary of the County Education Committee, stated that milking classes had been arranged in fifteen elementary schools during the previous spring and had proved very successful. He said that the boys employed had proven very useful during harvest-time. The Education Committee said they would happily allow the classes to take place again, but they would have to be at the farmers' own expense.

On Thursday, 10 February, Mr and Mrs W.J. Curtis of Burleigh,

Tom Wiltshire smoking a cigarette in France in 1916.

Linden Road, Gloucester, received official notification that their son, Private Sydney F. Curtis, of the 1st Battalion Scotts Guards, was killed in action on 24 October 1914. He had been reported missing since that date. An official correspondent said of Private Curtis:

*He was one of the dauntless few that lay amid a heap of German dead after the Battle of Loos which resulted in the capture of that village by the British and the military position known as Hill 70. He was one of a party of 80 told to hold a certain position at all costs, but they soon became isolated and it was clear to every man that there was no chance of saving themselves. They held their ground, however, until their last cartridge was spent and on the following morning were found dead with their bandoliers empty and the ground around them heaped with Germans.*

The *Gloucester Journal* reported:

*Private Curtis was an old Sir Thomas Rich's boy, was 28 years of age, and leaves a widow and a daughter born four months after his death. He was a great favourite among his comrades and his bright and cheerful disposition, under all circumstances, earned him the nickname of 'Happy.'*

The *Gloucester Journal* of Saturday, 12 February, reported that a Gloucester man had won the DCM. The story read:

*Private E. Harris, son of Mr and Mrs Harris, 22 Leonard Road, and whose home is at 158 Melbourne Street, a stretcher bearer of the 1st Gloucester Regiment, has been officially announced as recommended for the D.C.M. Pte. Harris was called up with the reserve men. He was working at the Wagon Works as a striker in the smiths' shop at the time and was one of the Works Ambulance Corps. He is an old Linden Road School boy and was one of the soccer football players of that school and also played this popular game with his regiment when stationed in India.*

Private E. Harris, a stretcher-bearer, was recommended for the DCM in February 1916. He was called up with the reserve men and had formerly been employed by the Wagon Works as a striker in the smiths' shop.

During February, Mr Hubert F. Fisher returned to England from Buenos Aires to offer his services to the government in the Royal Flying Corps. Fisher, the son of Mr John Fisher of Tudor House, Gloucester, had worked as the chief engineer and manager at Messrs Pedro Storm v Cia's machinery business from 1910, but

An enlistment poster stating: 'The Empire Needs Men!' Propaganda posters issued by the government urged men to enlist. Many were exempt due to their jobs. Many men claimed exemption because they worked on farms and some appealed as conscientious objectors, citing religious or moral reasons.

had resigned and had taken up aviation purely for patriotic purposes. He was awarded a pilot's diploma by the Aero Club of Argentina and possession of the certificate allowed him to enter straight into the Royal Naval Air Service or the Royal Flying Corps. He was the first Englishman to obtain a flying diploma in Argentina. His wife, who was also an aviator, insisted on returning to England to assist with the Red Cross or other useful work *'for the sake of the Old Country'*.

Compulsory enlistment for men between the ages of 18 and 41 was introduced for single men and childless widowers. However, essential war workers, clergymen, the physically unfit and approved conscientious

A Zeppelin preparing for flight. With the outbreak of war, Germany made great use of Zeppelins for reconnaissance and bombing raids. In 1910, they were first flown commercially by Deutsche Luftschiffahrts-AG (DELAG) and, by 1914, they had carried 34,000 pasengers on 1,500 separate flights.

Carl Hertz, an illusionist, who appeared at the Hippodrome in March 1916. The newspaper advert read: 'The mysterious always attracts and those who enjoy being thoroughly mystified will appreciate the chief turn at the Hippodrome this week. For 30 years, Carl Hertz, who hails from San Francisco, has been bewildering the public with his illusions.'

objectors were exempt. The upper age was later raised to 51.

On Thursday, 2 March, the wives, children and dependants of Gloucester postal workers, on active service, were treated to entertainment at the Corn Exchange. The proceedings commenced with tea, provided by Messrs J.A. Fisher and Son. The number of guests totalled 150, of which seventy were women and eighty were children. Staff of the post office and the telegraph and telephone department waited on the guests. The room was decorated with flags, while the platform displayed many palms and flowers as well as a roll of honour. The musical programme contained a pianoforte solo by Mr Shaw, the baritone voice of Mr Gunston, a toe dance by Miss Marie Rose, a violin solo by Miss D. Orchard as well as humorous items provided by Miss Lallie Hay and Mr Tom Hay. There was also a Punch and Judy show laid on for the children, with the operator being 'Professor' Alexander. After the show, the children were all given gifts.

The mayor and mayoress were present at the event as well as officials from the post office. The mayor paid tribute to the post office and said that the entertainment was excellent and served to keep up the spirits of wives and children of men away serving at the Front.

The Hippodrome announced its forthcoming entertainment in the *Gloucester Journal* of Saturday, 4 March:

*Enterprising as ever, the management of the Hippodrome, Gloucester, have secured the marvellous American illusionist Carl Hertz (he is a native of San Francisco) for next week, when he will have the assistance of Miss Emilie D'Alton, who is known as the beautiful vaudeville lady.*

*For the past 30 years, Carl Hertz has been mystifying the public with his giant illusions and wherever he has been, his efforts have always been appreciated. On this occasion, he will produce a 'War Map' dealing with the present crisis which ought to be seen by every loyal subject. A number of well-known London artistes will accompany Mr. Hertz and the programme promises to be one of the best put forward at this house of entertainment. Mr. Edwards, who is to be congratulated on securing such an attraction for his patrons, strongly advises the booking of seats well in advance. There will be no increase in prices.'*

On Wednesday, 22 March, George William Williams, licensee of the White Hart Inn in Bell Lane, appeared before the city's police court charged with supplying a wounded soldier with drink. The defendant pleaded not guilty.

Private Clarke of the Army Service Corps, who was a patient at the Hillfield Red Cross Hospital, stated that on 28 February, he had accompanied Privates Ray and Westall to the Parkend Empire. On leaving there, they proceeded to Bell Lane where they talked to a man who invited them to the White Hart for a drink. Clarke said he had three whiskeys, which were given to him by other people drinking in the inn. He said there were lots of people there but he did not recall seeing the defendant. He stated that the effect of the drinks made him quite drunk. The prosecutor pointed out that he was wearing a hospital armlet at the time.

**Emilie D'Alton, stage assistant to Carl Hertz. D'Alton appeared in many of Hertz's illusions including one where she appeared to be suspended in mid-air with no visible support. As well as Hertz's assistant, she was also his wife. Their show at the Hippodrome in March 1916 received rave reviews.**

In reply to Mr Lane, who was defending, Clarke said he did not know who had paid for the drink. He felt ashamed of himself and was aware that by having a drink he had got the landlord into serious trouble.

Nelson Bayliss, secretary of the Hillfield Red Cross Hospital, said he visited the defendant's house and spoke to him with reference to Clarke being served with drink. He was unable to trace the men who had paid for the drinks and understood that Clarke had been served through a small window, and it was possible that the person serving the drinks was unable to see the customer.

It was stated in court that the real culprits were the men who bought the drinks. The defendant said he would no more think of serving a wounded soldier than he would a drunken man.

The chairman stated it was a very serious charge and if the case had been proved that the licensee would have faced heavy penalties. Taking into account the defendant's good character and the possibility that he didn't know who the drink was handed to, the magistrates felt that justice would be served if the licensee would pay the prosecution costs. The case was then dismissed.

During March, several tradesmen in the city were brought before the police court charged with failing to obscure the lights within their premises. Most defendants pleaded guilty and apologised and were fined 10 shillings. With regards to Ernest Baldwin of the King's Arms in Hare Lane, Inspector Butt said that the lights complained about were at the back of the house and difficult to get to. There were seven windows and a skylight unprotected. The defendant had twice been warned before. The chairman said this was a particularly bad case and fined Baldwin 15 shillings.

The chairman reminded defendants that they had rendered themselves liable to a penalty of £100.

On Wednesday, 29 March, a meeting of the Gloucester Military Tribunal was held at the Guildhall during the afternoon. The mayor (Sir James Bruton) presided.

A local firm of toy and game makers applied for postponement for six of their employees. It had been arranged earlier that all six cases would be held together. The firm had already seen fifty of its workers enlist and appealed for the six men who they described as *'absolutely indispensable'*. It was stated that if the men were taken then parts of the factory would have to be closed. The military stated that it was far more important to win the war than the export of goods should be maintained. The tribunal granted postponement on three of the cases until 30 September, two were postponed until 30 June, and the remaining case was postponed until 30 April.

The *Gloucester Journal* of 1 April reported the disappointment felt when the circus failed to arrive in the city:

*Tuesday's blizzard, which caused so much damage in many parts of England and many delays, was responsible for the disappointment occasioned by the non-appearance in Gloucester on Thursday – the day announced for its visit – of Sangers' Circus. This all-British institution has been a welcome visitor to Gloucester for many years and it is satisfactory that the visit has only been delayed and not abandoned. On Monday next, April 3rd, the Kingsholm Ground will be alive with the many delights which are attached to Lord John Sangers' Royal Circus and Menagerie and Gloucester people will have another opportunity of indulging in the thrills and laughter which the fearless riders and comic clowns of Sangers' are so adept at providing. One of the features of the entertainment will be the brilliant and fearless exhibition of riding by the 'Great Russian Cossack Troupe' who will give peasant dances, ground manoeuvres and a realistic representation*

*of the way in which the men of our Russian Ally fight the Germans.
It is stated that these wonderful riders are not circus performers
but are the pick of Russia's finest horsemen who are unfortunately
debarred from taking their part in the great European conflict. The
circus will also include Pimpo's greatest absurdity, a most
laughable production in which the two Willies introduce the Turk
to the British Lion and Pimpo exhibits his ship of the desert. The
beautiful Della Cassa Sisters give an interesting exhibition with
three elephants and three horses; while a pair of pure white twin
horses are led by 'Franscesca' in a riding and driving
performance. Other star turns are the Ariel Danes and the
performing sea lions.*

During April, Mr H. David reported that a further £3 3s-worth of tobacco
and cigarettes had been dispatched to soldiers at the Front. Payment
came from the tobacco fund of Messrs Moreland's Match Works
employees and staff. Another 36 gross of matches was also given by the
firm.

A meeting discussing the work of women on the land was reported in
the *Gloucester Journal* of Saturday, 15 April. It read:

*A meeting of the County War Agriculture Committee was held at
the Shire Hall, Gloucester, on Saturday afternoon, Mr M. W.
Colchester-Wemyss (chairman) presiding.*

*The report of the Women's Labour Sub-Committee was
presented by Miss Deane who said of the 20 districts in the county
all, with the exception of four, had appointed women
representatives and registrars for all villages in their areas. The
canvass, so far as it had gone, was very promising. It showed that
a large number of skilled women who had done farm work in the
past were willing to do so again; while there was a large number
of women who could give a few hours service a day; and there was
a certain number of women and girls who desired to be trained.
The reports were very satisfactory from some parishes.*

*A circular letter was read from the Board of Agriculture with
regard to the redistribution of agricultural labour, pointing out
how in certain districts, some farms were carrying their ordinary
staffs while in other cases the labour was so much depleted that it
was almost impossible to carry on the farms.*

An announcement in the *Gloucester Journal* of Saturday, 29 April read:

*The Gloucester Rural War Agricultural Committee urge that a
great effort should now be made throughout the rural district to*

*diminish the quantity of sparrows, wood pigeons and starlings by taking nests and otherwise, and also to get rid of rats and mice.*

The May meeting of the Gloucestershire Farmers' Union took place at the City Chambers in Gloucester and was presided over by Mr J.H. Alpass. Mr W. Pearce Ellis, explaining his late arrival at the meeting, stated that he had just attended a meeting in a nearby city regarding agriculture and recruiting. There, the following had been agreed to:

1. The military representative shall not appeal against one man being left to a farm for every team of horses worked on that farm.

2. One man shall be left for every twenty cows where there is assistance given in milking.

3. One man shall be left for every twelve cows where there is no assistance given in milking.

4. One man shall be left for every fifty head of stall-fed cattle.

5. One man shall be left for every 200 sheep not less than 6 months old.

6. Blacksmiths and wheelwrights should be exempt so far as the military authorities are concerned.

7. No thatchers to be taken.

8. No manager of a stud farm, or herdsmen in charge of pedigree herds to be taken.

9. When a farmer is of military age, he must take the place of a man with cattle or sheep.

The chairman stated that the advisory committees, in conjunction with the military representatives, should take note of the nine points mentioned so that no man should need to come before a tribunal who is essential to the working of a farm. Mr Mutton went on to say that Sir Sydney Olivier, permanent under secretary to the Board of Agriculture, had assured him that if the Farmers' Union experienced any difficulty with a military officer in a *bona fide* case, that he would give the union every support if the case was appealed immediately.

Regular meetings of the Gloucester Military Tribunal were held at the Guildhall to decide who should be exempted from enlistment. At a meeting on 24 May, many men applied for postponement and covered a range of professions including a butchers, travelling salesmen, a ship's mate, carters, firemen, drapers, brushmakers, bakers, grocers, cellarmen and a corn and fodder contractor. Most cases had their call into the army postponed to a later date. The firemen were considered a reserved occupation and were therefore exempt. However, a draper's traveller, aged 19, had his application refused.

Weekly lists appeared in the local newspaper of British casualties,

An advert for National War Bonds. An advert that appeared in April 1916 urged people to purchase war bonds. It read: 'Lend your money to your country. The soldier does not grudge offering his life to his country. He offers it freely, for his life may be the price of Victory. But Victory cannot be won without money as well as men, and your money is needed. Unlike the soldier, the investor runs no risk. If you invest in Exchequer Bonds your money, capital and interest alike, is secured on the Consolidated Fund of the United Kingdom, the premier security of the world.'

**Your**

**Thankoffering**

for

**VICTORY**

Buy National War Bonds. It is your duty, your privilege, your best thank-offering to the men who have fought and won

including those killed, wounded and missing. The *Gloucester Journal* of Saturday, 27 May, showed that the previous Friday's list included the names, all from the Gloucester Regiment, of seventy-five officers (twenty-two were killed) and 1,553 rank and file (247 dead, 1,306 wounded and missing).

In June, a meeting was held on behalf of the British and Foreign Sailors' Society in Southgate Lecture Hall presided over by the mayor, Sir James Bruton. The meeting opened with a verse of the National Anthem.

The event was reported in the *Gloucester Journal* of Saturday, 10 June, and the death of Lord Kitchener, on 5 June, was discussed. The article read:

*The Mayor said they were met under the shadow of a great sorrow that evening. He did not know of anything that had caused such a shock as the news received that afternoon of the loss of the* Hampshire. *It was a terribly sad blow to this country. When they thought what Lord Kitchener had done, they would see what a serious thing it was for England. Death comes to all, and they may be*

Field Marshall Horatio Herbert Kitchener, 1st Earl Kitchener, played a central role in the early part of the First World War. In 1914, he became the secretary of state for war and organised the largest voluntary army the world had ever seen. His face appeared on endless recruitment posters. However, he died on 5 June 1916, long before the war ended.

**An advert for Bird's blancmange, which appeared in the *Gloucester Journal* of Saturday, 10 June 1916. The advert stated that it was a dish that was hard to beat ideal for 'Soldier Sam' serving out in France.**

*sure he met his fate in the same spirit that he had faced death many a time on the battlefield. There was no more appropriate time to urge the claims of such a society as the British and Foreign Sailors' Society. Referring to the recent naval battle, Sir James said he was sure that the sole aim of every man who took part therein was to serve his country. They filled everyone with admiration. He was compelled to think that if there was a society which appealed to them at the present time, it was the society in whose name they were met that night.*

*Bishop Frodsham, in referring to the news that had been received that afternoon, said that he rose to speak with profound feeling. Perhaps he was the only one present in that room who had known Lord Kitchener personally. He (Bishop Frodsham) was one of the first to welcome him and Lieut. Col. Fitzgerald when they landed in Australia. He could testify to the humility of Lord Kitchener and the love and respect he had aroused in all parts of the Empire. No-one would feel his death more clearly than the working man.*

The Gloucester Journal of 10 June reported on the case of a postman who had appeared before the Gloucester City Petty Sessions accused of stealing items from the mail. Harry Lidiard, age 44, was charged with stealing a letter containing two 10s notes, a postal order for 5s 6d, as well as six penny stamps.

The court heard that, after several complaints of undelivered mail, an investigating officer had arrived from London and made up a test letter which included the missing items. The envelope was marked with invisible ink. The letter was undelivered and was later found, open, at the accused's address.

Mr Wellington, prosecuting, said that other complaints had been received regarding missing postal orders. When detained, the accused

**Women look for news of their men. Wives and mothers eagerly scanned any notices posted containing lists of casualties. A crowd would gather when any new news was issued. Daily columns of deceased and wounded servicemen also appeared in local newspapers.**

had the marked notes on his person. It was stated that the postman had worked for the post office for twenty years and had a clean record but, due to illness, his family had become reliant on moneylenders. The defendant pleaded guilty to the charges.

Mr Lane, defending, suggested that the bench should take the same course that they had in other cases brought by the post office, whereby, if the accused was of military age, he should be bound over on the understanding that he joined the army.

The bench, taking in the defendant's previous good character, agreed to the suggestion.

As the Battle of the Somme raged in Europe, relatives back in Gloucester dreaded the knock on the door, as they had throughout the war, of the telegram boy bringing news of their loved ones' death. Newspapers carried the news of all wounded and killed soldiers.

On 2 July, the Gloucester Friendly and Trade Societies' Church Parade, an annual event, took place. The numbers attending the meeting were down on previous years, with many men away fighting in the war. The parade included the Wagon Works Silver Band, a detachment of the St John Ambulance Brigade and male and female members of the various friendly and trade societies in the city. They were marshalled at the Spa and proceeded by way of Park Road and the Barton Gates to the Guildhall, where they were met by the mayor and officials as well as a posse of police. From the Guildhall, the parade proceeded to the

**Tom Wiltshire, holding a ladle, pictured with civilians, including a RAMC man on the left and elderly civilian on the right, at camp.**

**The Gloucester Regiment relaxing at camp. In the background are the many white tents that accommodated the troops.**

cathedral, where there was a large congregation awaiting them.

The *Gloucester Journal* of 8 July reported on the enrolment of the Gloucester Volunteer Corps. The article read:

> *The Gloucester Volunteer Corps paraded 225 strong (inclusive of the cadets) at the Kingsholm Headquarters on Thursday evening and marched, under the command of Mr. H.G. Norman and with a full complement of officers, to the Guildhall in order to take the enrolment oath under the Volunteer act of 1863 and in accordance with the new regulations issued by the Army Council.*
>
> *At the Guildhall, the Mayor, the City High Sheriff, the Town Clerk and a number of alderman and councillors were in waiting in the Council Chamber to receive the volunteers.*

In a letter to Mrs L. Jones, of 28 Twyver Street, Gloucester, an officer wrote that her son, Leonard, had met with an unfortunate accident. The officer wrote:

> *The accident has caused him, I am afraid, the loss of the thumb and one finger of his left hand. I am more dreadfully sorry about it than I can say. The accident was caused by the explosion of a fuse which he was holding in his hand; how exactly it happened he*

*will, I expect, be more competent to tell you than I can. I was about 50 yards away from him when it happened. Leonard was splendidly plucky over it and stood like a Briton while we bandaged up his hands (they were both damaged). I'm afraid he won't be fit for service with the guns again without his fingers, which will be a great disappointment for him and for all his many friends in the*

**Wounded troops on board a train receive refreshments. Here, the walking wounded return to camp via a train with a stop on the way to receive a welcome drink. The more seriously wounded faced long, tortuous journeys to crowded casualty centres before they were returned home.**

*Battery, including myself. Your son has been in my section for well over a year and I can unhesitatingly say that there is not a man of them that I would have been sorrier to lose. Will you accept on his behalf the heartfelt sympathies which all his pals extend to him?*

The *Birmingham Daily Post* of 18 August carried the story of a drowned soldier and chauffeur. The story read:

*About half past eleven on Wednesday night, an Australian soldier, since identified as Bernard Browning, son of Mr. Albert Browning of Severn Farm, Quedgeley, near Gloucester, who was home on sick leave, called at Mr. Walter Colwell's, the Spa Mews, Gloucester, and chartered a taxi-cab to take him home after spending the evening in the city with some friends. To get to Severn Farm, the Gloucester and Berkeley Canal had to be crossed at Rea Bridge, between three and four miles from Gloucester and it is stated that the driver of the taxi-cab, Frank Lippiatt, whose home is at Ross, was cautioned by his employer to be careful in regard to this bridge.*

*As the chauffeur did not return to the garage with the taxi-cab, enquiries were set on foot and yesterday morning indications were found of the motor-car having been driven into the canal close to Rea Bridge, the stone-work at the approach to which was damaged. There were obvious motor-car wheel marks in the direction of the water's edge and some petrol was seen floating on the surface of the canal in the vicinity of the bridge. Dragging operations were carried out yesterday morning and shortly after noon, the taxi-cab was raised, by means of a crane, sufficiently above the water for the body of Browning to be recovered from inside the taxi. As the cab was lifted, the body of the driver fell back into the water. The body of the cab collapsed as it was being hoisted but half an hour later, the chassis was secured. Dragging operations were resumed and the body of Lippiatt was recovered in the course of the afternoon.*

*The deceased soldier left Quedgeley for Australia some six years ago and, upon the outbreak of war, enlisted in the Australian Force. He served through the Dardanelles campaign and, after being in Egypt for a short time, was transferred to France. He was invalided home and, after being in hospital for some time, was allowed a fortnight's sick leave. He had presented himself for further service but after medical examination was sent home again for a further period of fourteen days.*

During September, the suggestion for a club for wounded soldiers in

Gloucester was made. Bishop Frodsham, the chairman of the club, along with the mayor, Sir James Bruton, visited the Red Cross Hospitals in the area and explained to the men the purpose of the club and asked for their co-operation.

Bishop Frodsham later received a letter from the Gloucestershire Branch of the Red Cross, which read:

> *Please accept the heartiest thanks of the Gloucestershire Branch of the British Red Cross Society for your most welcome offer of a club for the use of the invalid soldiers in Gloucester during the winter months. Nothing could be more acceptable, as after the time is over when garden parties and such entertainments are possible, there is nothing whatever for the men to do and a club, such as you offer, will be of the greatest value in every respect.*
>
> *Yours sincerely,*
> *F. Colchester-Wemyss.*

After an appeal in the *Gloucester Journal*, a donation for £5 was received from the Gloucester branch of the Girls' Friendly Society as well as gifts of a bagatelle table and a billiard table. Alderman Braine offered to loan all the glass, china and cutlery needed for the canteen.

The newspaper wrote:

> *If the citizens generally follow these splendid leads with contributions in cash or otherwise, the committee will be able to open the club well equipped with the necessaries and we hope some extra comforts of a first-class club for the wounded Tommies during their stay in our city. It may be pointed out that everything is to be provided free for the soldiers (who get no pay whilst in hospital), so that chests of tea, cases of coffee (essence) and cocoa, tins of biscuits, cakes, etc., will be very acceptable contributions; but Tommy has been promised on good authority that he shall NOT be offered JAM! Until the club is opened, all communications should be addressed: The Hon. Secretaries, Tommy's Own Club, 20 Clarence Street.*

In October, Mr and Mrs W.H. Lane, of 5 Priory Place, Greyfriars, Gloucester, received a letter from their son, Lance-Corporal H.W. Lane of the Grenadier Guards, notifying them that he had been awarded the DCM for gallant conduct in the storming of Lesboeufs. He wrote:

> *I have received heaps of congratulations and also drank a fine drop of Scotch with the Company officers. There is a cash consideration attached to this medal – the second highest it is possible for an*

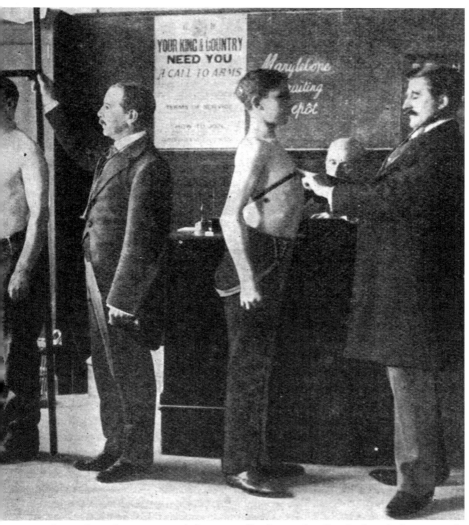

**A youth and a man receiving a medical examination before being passed fit to enlist. In the background is a recruitment poster stating, 'Your King and country need you.'**

*N.C. officer or man to win. I am feeling in the pink at present and hope to remain so. It looks like another winter here but 'Bill' must know he's up against it now. Of course, he's mad but he will have to give the game up sooner or later because we will simply smash him up if he continues to hang on. We lost some good lads in the last battle but 'Bill' didn't get off scot free. Well, I've been through a few battles now – Neuve Chapelle, Aubers Ridge, Festubert, Loos, Ginchy and Lesboeufs – not so bad to get through safely, is it! May my good luck continue.*

*In less than a fortnight, I shall have been out here two years – rather a good record, isn't it? It is getting very cold now; sharp frost this morning but it's better than the rain.*

The *Gloucester Journal* of 4 November announced the opening of a new club for women munition workers at the Institute, Southgate Street. The opening ceremony was performed by the Duchess of Beaumont. Also present were the mayor and mayoress, the high sheriff as well as several councillors and guests. The lord bishop, presiding, said that he welcomed the club and was sure it would be of great interest to munition workers throughout the city. He congratulated the Duchess of Beaumont for all her work putting the club together. The duchess responded by saying that all credit should be given to Mrs Cyril Ward, whose idea it was in the first place.

Refreshments were served at the opening, which were followed by a concert that included Mr Julian Kimbell, who had appeared previously at Covent Garden and the London Royal Opera.

An appeal for Christmas gifts appeared in the *Gloucester Journal* of Saturday, 16 December. It read:

*We desire very heartily to commend to our readers, at this season of kindly thoughts and good deeds, the effort of the Voluntary Aid Red Cross Hospitals in the City to obtain the greatest possible number and variety of gifts for our wounded soldiers. We may give in money or in kind. The idea to have a Pound and Christmas Gift day is excellent and we are quite sure there will be a most generous response on the part of the public. Today (Saturday) all of us will have an opportunity, according to our means (for we will take the inclination for granted in a cause so elequent) of sending something to the hospitals. A pound of cake, a pot of jam, a basket of fruit, a hamper of vegetable, cigarettes, tobacco – it does not matter what we send, it will be welcome as giving pleasure to those who have earned practical expression of our thanks and gratitude. For the most part, what is asked for can be given with the least sacrifice on the part of the donors; but if some sacrifice has to be made the appeal should be as generously responded to, for such a gift, like Mercy, is twice blessed. If any of our readers have up to this point been undecided as to whether they should give or as to what they shall give, let us resolve their doubts at once by saying*

When a deadlock was reached at the Western Front during Christmas 1916, it was possible, for the first time, to give the men Christmas leave. A spell at the Front, where spending was impossible, meant the soldiers had accrued a nice balance of pay, even though they only received 1s. 1d. a day. They were said to spend generously, many buying toy animals for their children back home.

*that anything will be acceptable which will add variety to hospital diet and make the lives of those who have suffered wounds and hardships for our sakes happier at this season of year. It is not, in truth, a Christmas of peace and good-will according to the old standard of tradition; but the spirit of Christmas must be kept alive and in no way can we better do this than by responding generously to the appeal for the Hospitals Pound Day.*

A Boxing Day rugby football match held at Kingsholme between Gloucester and Cinderford raised £61 6s for the Palace Red Cross Hospital. Further charity matches were planned for 1917.

## *Chapter Four*

# 1917 – Seeing it Through

A well-attended meeting of the Gloucestershire War Agricultural Committee took place at the Shire Hall in Gloucester on the afternoon of Saturday, 13 January. It was agreed that seventeen prisoners-of-war would cultivate land for potatoes in the neighbourhood of Park End. The committee had been corresponding with the War Office to see if another gang of prisoners could be sent to cultivate land at Pope's Hill, but this depended on whether accommodation could be arranged for the men.

It was decided at the meeting that a survey would take place to see what land was available to grow home produce in the area. The question of the supply and high cost of seed potato was also discussed.

The *Gloucester Journal* of Saturday, 20 January, reported the death of a local soldier who had been killed on the previous Christmas Eve:

> *Mrs Herbert Hunt of 238 Barton Street, Gloucester, has received a letter from Captain G. L. Davy, Gloucestershire Regiment, giving details as to how her son, Private Morgan H. Hunt, was killed on Christmas Eve. In the course of his letter, Capt. Davy says: 'He was a very good fellow and I know how very sorry Capt. Tubbs*

**The Land Army was set up in Great Britain in 1917. Women played a big role in agricultural work and were asked to sign on for either six months or a year. With many men away fighting, they provided a vital service.**

**Soldiers relax at a military hospital while listening to gramophone records and playing cards.**

*will be when he hears about it. Your son was out with me only an hour before he was hit. He helped to take two German prisoners at the time. He was very plucky and did not appear to be in great pain. We all hoped and thought he would live.'*

*Deceased, who was 19 years of age, was formerly employed at the Hatherley Step Works, Gloucester. His father is also serving in France.*

On Saturday, 3 February, the Gloucester Co-operative and Industrial Society held a party for wounded soldiers at the Gloucester Red Cross Hospital. The entertainment took place at the Society's Lecture Hall in Brunswick Road and included a concert and tea. Cigarettes were handed around and Mr R.J. Templeman, who was master of ceremonies, extended a cordial welcome on behalf of the society. He extended his sympathies and wished the men a speedy and complete recovery. The concert included songs, recitations, tambourine and bones duets, humorous songs and a pianoforte solo. After the programme, a 'meat tea' was served and Private Levy expressed the appreciation of all the men who attended. He spoke very highly of the people who contributed to the enjoyable programme. His comments were met with three cheers.

Mr Templeman responded by saying they had derived great pleasure from entertaining the men and that it was their duty to do all they could to relieve the monotony of those who had been wounded 'doing their bit' for the country.

On 24 March, the *Yellowstone News* in Montana carried the headline 'U.S. expected to announce that state of war exists'. The newspaper went on to report that: *'News received from Plymouth that fifteen men, some of them Americans, had been drowned when the American merchantmen* Vigilancia *was sunk without warning by a German submarine.'* The story also stated: *'President Wilson is expected, within 48 hours, to indicate definitely that he believes a virtual state of war exists between the United States and Germany.'*

On 5 April, the *Evening Herald* reported:

*The U.S. Senate has passed the resolution declaring a state of war with Germany by 82 votes to 6 at 11.15pm after 13 hours continuous debate. There was no demonstration when the result was announced.*

America joined the war on 6 April 1917.

The West of England Joint Executive Committee, for training and treatment of disabled soldiers and sailors, met during April. It was decided, provided that the Ministry of Pensions approved, that classes should be opened to retrain disabled men in various skills including bootmaking, switchboard attendant work, tailoring, clerical work, plumbing, gas fitting and motor car engineering. It was agreed that men should also be sent to the cloth mills of Messrs Apperley, Curtis and Co of Stroud to be retrained.

At a council meeting in late April, the damage caused by starlings was discussed. The story was reported in the *Gloucester Journal*:

*It was decided to apply to the Home Secretary for a renewal for a period of two years of the order depriving the starling of protection under the Wild Birds Protection Acts.*

*Major-General N.F.U. Sampson-Way, C.B., suggested that the starling did more good than harm on the land.*

*Mr. J. H Alpass, however, said that opinion was absolutely opposed to the view of the large body of agriculturists in the county.*

*Mr. G.E. Lloyd-Baker said he understood the view of farmers was that starlings did not do much harm until they became so numerous as they had done of late, when as vegetarians, they had proved very destructive to crops. That was exactly the point. Up to*

*a certain stage, the starlings were innocuous but they had
multiplied considerably.*

*Mr. H. Dent-Brocklehurst hoped the indiscriminate slaughter of
'my friend the starling' would be avoided. Regard must be had to
what he described as the balance of nature in these matters. There
was no doubt that a large number of birds were most valuable
insecticides.*

*The council thought that to renew the order for two years in the
case of the starling would be sufficient.*

The *Cheltenham Chronicle* of Saturday, 28 April, reported the death of
a young soldier:

*Mrs Phelps, of 5 Portland Street, London Road, Gloucester, has
received official information that her son, Pte. James Phelps,
Gloucester Regt., has died of wounds. The deceased soldier, who
was only 19 years of age, was mobilised at the outbreak of war in
August 1914. He served in France for some months and was sent
to England with frost-bitten feet. After rejoining his regiment, he
was drafted to the East. When war broke out, he was employed as
a painter for Mr. Laider, Gloucester.*

A reader wrote to the *Gloucester Journal* of 5 May complaining abouth
the 'amusement tax'. His letter read:

*Sir, I do not like rushing into print, but as an entertainer of over 45
years myself (Poole's Myrioramas being founded in 1837), I feel I
must enter my protest against the increased tax on amusement-
goers. Granted that amusements, like alcohol and tobacco, are a
luxury, i.e., can be done without, I claim that amusements are a
necessary luxury. Mr. Bonar Law himself says 'that they had a real
psychological value at a time like this, for people could not always
be brooding and there must be a means of forgetting.'*

*If the places of amusement are closed we shall have to double
the police to keep order in the streets, etc. My present complaint is
that the proposed tax again hits the poor hardest. The price of
commodities has increased. Take oatmeal, which was 2½d before
the war, is now 8d. per lb., and we are advised to eat it to save
bread. Now the poor have only so much money to spend on luxuries
(beer, 'baccy and amusement) where there are large families and
only so much left after paying for necessaries. To nearly double
the price of amusement means that some of the family must go
without, and to charge 2d on a 3d ticket is to my mind iniquitous.*

*Again, those in sedentary occupations cannot afford the extra charges, as in many cases their salaries have not been raised. Everything connected with amusements has been raised in price, yet we dare not raise our prices of admission, knowing the public will not stand it, so the Government steps in and puts up to a lot of extra work and cost to collect money for them by taxing amusements too much.*

*I notice the Chancellor says he does not tax many things because the cost of collection would be more than the income and staffs can not be procured. A very easy way to raise millions annually would be to tax bicycles. The tax for amusements will run the war from five to six hours a year only. The bicycle tax can be taken out at the Post Office like a dog license, and if any extra help is needed, some of the other departments where work is very short and light could help. For many years users of bicycles have stated they would welcome a bicycle license because it would give them the right to complain of the state of the roads in some districts, and today they are used to avoid excessive train and tram fares, and so go scot free.*

*By all means tax complimentary tickets; it will not be objected to. When the first tax was imposed, many quite expected they would have to pay and offered the money but it was not legal to take it. Leave the tax on the 3d. at 1d. and other prices at proportionate rates.*

*Yours etc.,*

*C. W. Poole.*

*Palace Theatre, Gloucester.*

*N.B. If a bicycle tax is introduced I would suggest that tricycles, and other machines used for wounded soldiers, sailors, invalids and cripples be exempt.*

On Saturday, 19 May, the *Gloucester Journal* told the story of the experience of local men onboard the *Arcadian*. The story read:

*Survivors of the transport Arcadian, torpedoed and sunk a month ago, have just returned home. All the officers were saved, with the exception of the second Marconi man. The survivors say the force of the explosion brought the wireless down so that the operators could not send out any more signals of distress, but he stuck to his position to the last and was standing by the machine with the receivers in his hand when the ship sank. Captain Willett went down on the bridge but he was picked up by a raft.*

*Sec.-Lieut. Lindsay Vears was on board the* Arcadian *when she was torpedoed and was picked up and taken to hospital at Malta. Since then he has proceeded on his journey.*

*Mr. and Mrs. O. A. Poole, St. Michael's Square, have received a letter from their son, Lance-Corpl. E. Poole, now in hospital at Malta, suffering from shock and cold from exposure. After eleven hours in an open boat, himself and 50 of his comrades were picked up by an English destroyer. Fortunately, a calm sea prevailed and they were safely landed and well cared for in hospital.*

*Pte. F. Ellis, who was on the torpedoed liner, in a letter to his mother (Mrs. W. E. Ellis, 61 Stroud Road) from a Malta hospital, says 'We were out in a little boat for eight hours before being picked up by a mine-sweeper. The boat kept filling with water but we baled it out with our boots. I only had my shirt and trousers on. It was pitch dark when we were picked up. The Navy chaps were good to us I thought my time had come. I shall not forget the experience as long as I live.' Pte. Elis was twice invalided on active service in France, being wounded once and, on another occasion, suffering from shell shock, which necessitated seven months' detention in hospital. His father, who is in the Navy, was in the Falkland Islands battle and has seen service in various parts of the world. Recently, he was invalided to England. Two brothers are in the Gloucesters.*

An open air meeting was held at the Spa Cricket Field on the evening of Thursday, 21 June, on behalf of the Gloucester Food Economy Campaign. Before the meeting took place, a selection of music was played by the Wagon Works Silver Band. Mr C.A.A. Fletcher, from the Ministry of Food, was the principal speaker. The committee was disappointed with efforts made to induce people to economise on their consumption of bread. Results showed that there was only a reduction of 6 per cent instead of the 20 per cent required. It was stated that one of the causes was undoubtedly the shortage of potatoes but, as the chairman pointed out, it was thought that many people didn't realise the grave situation in which Great Britain found itself regarding the shortage of food.

GLOUCESTERSHIRE
**War Agricultural Executive Committee.**

**NOTICE TO FARMERS.**

From the 14th June, NO MAN who is engaged whole time on a farm or farm work of National Importance IS TO BE POSTED FOR MILITARY SERVICE, or to be called up for Medical Examination or Re-examination.

Men receiving Notices should communicate at once with the Organising Surveyor, County Buildings, College Court, Gloucester.

(Signed) H. DENT-BROCKLEHURST, Chairman of the Executive Committee.

**A notice to farmers from the War Agricultural Executive Committee, which appeared in the** *Gloucester Journal* **of Saturday, 23 June 1917.**

The *Gloucester Journal* of Saturday, 23 June, carried the story of an Australian solder charged with bigamy:

> *Following upon a communication from the Gloucester police, the Metropolitan Police arrested Private Samuel Driggett, aged 27, of the Australian Imperial Force, on a charge of committing bigamy.*
>
> *The prisoner was brought up at the Marylebone Police Court on Thursday and was formally accused of intermarrying Mabel Florence Townsend, of 58 Grafton Road, Kentish Town, at St. Barnabas Church, Kentish Town, on 28th May last, his lawful wife, Julie Driggett, of 8 Park Road, Gloucester, whom he married at the Parish Church of Melksham, Wilts, on the 29th January last, being then and now alive.*
>
> *Miss Townsend, a well-dressed and pre-possessing young woman, evidently felt her position acutely when called to give evidence. She said she went through the ceremony of marriage with the prisoner on the 28th May and had lived with him for about a month at Grafton Road, Kentish Town. He described himself in the marriage certificate as a bachelor, and represented himself as such, and it was only when she was called to the Police Station on Wednesday that she heard that he had previously been married.*
>
> *Detective-Sergeant Page stated that on receipt of a communication from the Gloucester police he made inquiries, and arrested the prisoner the previous afternoon at the Crystal Palace. In reply to the charge, the prisoner said: 'Yes, it is quite true. I don't want any fuss. I shall be glad to get it over.'*
>
> *The accused was remanded and was granted permission to see his wife before he went to prison if she cared to see him.*

VAD nurses aid an injured soldier. With the ever-rising amount of casualties arriving back in Britain, there was a great need for assistance at hospitals. Thousands of women answered the call and became part of the Voluntary Aid Detachment (VAD), which aided injured soldiers, sailors and airmen.

Nine boys appeared at a children's court at Gloucester on Wednesday, 11 July, accused of stealing produce, worth 3 shillings, from allotments at

Tredworth. The oldest boy didn't appear and a boy who said he went to the allotments to fetch his brother was discharged. The other boys admitted the offence. The offence was regarded as very serious and a lot of damage had been done to the allotments by the boys. Richard Cook, the owner of the allotment raided, said that he caught the boys picking peas and pulling up carrots. The oldest boy ran away, as he had done on previous occasions, and no-one could catch him.

The chairman of the court said that the case was a serious matter and that many people working on the allotments were growing produce to provide food for the country and, in many cases, it was used to feed members of the army. A fine of 5 shillings was imposed on the boys and a fine of 10 shillings on the older boy, who was considered the ringleader. The chairman stated that any further similar cases would be treated far more severely.

The *Gloucester Journal* of Saturday, 14 July, reported the story of a suicide in the city under the headline *'Gloucester Soldier's Wife's Sad End'*. The story read:

> *The Divisional Coroner, Mr. John Waghorne, held an inquest at the Shire Hall, Gloucester, on Wednesday afternoon, on the body of Mrs. Annie Miriam Garlick, 69 Rosebery Avenue, a soldier's wife, whose body was recovered from the Gloucester and Berkeley Canal at Hempsted on Monday.*
>
> *The Coroner said the deceased woman was 36 years of age and her husband was at the present time serving in Salonika. Previous to joining the Army, her husband was a linesman in the employ of the post office. For some time, the deceased had been suffering from fits of depression and had been attended by Dr. St. Johnston. It seemed that on Saturday last she was out with a neighbour (Mrs. Barnett) to whom from time to time she had said that there was not much worth living for in this world. She seemed very depressed. On Sunday morning last she told her little boy to go and unlock the coal-house door and while he was away she left the house and had not since been seen alive. Inquiries were made and her absence was reported to the police. Nothing was heard of her until Monday morning, when the bridgeman at Sims' Bridge, Hempsted, was shouted to by some men who were proceeding up the canal on a tugboat and told that the body of a woman was seen to rise to the top of the water near the bend. The bridgeman went to the spot indicated and found the body and secured it to the bank. About 20 yards away, a hat and mackintosh were found on the bank. P.C.*

*Powell was called to the spot, and had since made inquiries, but no letter or message was found on deceased's body or at her house. There were no circumstances to explain why she went to the canal and there were no signs of violence on the body. He understood that there was no real reason for her to have worried apart from the fact that her mother's death earlier in the year had depressed her. On the previous Tuesday morning, she had received a very cheerful letter from her husband and certainly not one to have a depressing effect on her.*

*The Coroner said their sympathy went out to the husband, who would receive such sad news whilst away fighting for his country, also with the two young children, left without father or mother to look after them. The jury concurred.*

At the beginning of August, three cases appeared before Colonel Curtis Hayward at the Gloucester County Petty Sessions.

Harry Poynter Woodward was summoned to the court but did not appear. He was charged with failing to send his child, aged 11, to school and was fined 5 shillings in his absence.

Frederick Oswald was summoned for being in possession of matches at a munitions factory. The defendant pleaded guilty and said it was an oversight due to his jacket getting wet through and him having to change it. The chairman stated that the bench always took a dim view of cases where matches were carried close to munitions and the defendant was sentenced to a month in prison.

Frederick Burgess and Osborne Macey were both charged with being in possession of a piece of a cigarette while at a munitions factory. Both men were fined £1.

On the morning of Friday, 3 August, two gangs of boys, aged between 11 and 15, were brought before the Children's Court charged with trespassing on the Great Western Railway and exposing themselves to danger. The members of the two gangs, who had called themselves Germans and Russians, all pleaded guilty to the charges. Mr P.W. Pine, prosecuting for the railway company, said that the offence took place in the vicinity of St Catherine's meadows. One gang had managed to get on the line and was throwing stones at the gang below. The boys had also thrown stones at allotment holders and trains had to be stopped because of them. The court said that it took the matter very seriously but it praised the boys for owning up to their wrongdoing. Each defendant was fined 5 shillings.

In August, the quartermaster of the 3rd Battalion GVR, camped at

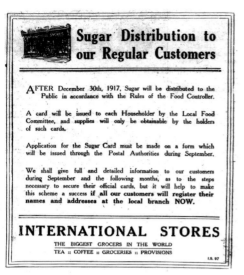

**An advert from International Stores regarding sugar distribution to regular customers. The advert appeared in the *Gloucester Journal* on Saturday, 1 September 1917.**

Sneedham's Green, wrote to the *Gloucester Journal* wishing its readers well and requesting *'presents of green vegetables (peas, beans, cabbages etc.) and of salads (lettuce, tomatoes etc.) to supplement the men's army rations while in camp from August 4th to August 11th'*. The gifts could be delivered to the Saracen's Head Hotel in Eastgate Street, where they would be received by Mr J. Hanman before being taken to the camp.

The *Gloucester Journal* at the beginning of September reported a presentation to a Gloucester DCM holder. The story read:

*A pleasing function took place on the premises of the Gloucester Shirt Company Ltd., on Tuesday morning, when Drummer Harold Farmer, who is home on leave from France and who was married last week, was made the recipient of a dinner service, subscribed for by his fellow employees, and an oaken timepiece, suitably inscribed, presented him by the Directors of the Company, in commemoration of his having won the D.C.M. in France for gallantry in action on the 5th April, 1917. Mr. Acton made the presentation on behalf of the employees and Mr. George W. Brace for the Directors. The recipient feelingly acknowledged the gifts. It is interesting to note that out of the Gloucester Shirt Company's staff of 31 men, of military age when hostilities commenced, 24 have at various dates been called up for service, of whom one has been killed, one discharged and four wounded. Farmer was with the company for seven years, coming as a boy. He was a member of the Choral Society and Voluntary Choir at the Cathedral.*

On Saturday, 8 September, a sports event, organised in connection with the Wagon Works, was held at the Kingsholm Football Ground. There was a good attendance and 5,000 people passed through the gates. Before the commencement of the events, a fancy dress competition took place, which included eighty competitors from the works. All proceeds from the event went to the Gloucestershire Royal Infirmary, with collections being made in the street, which included a collecting pony, ladies in fancy dress and the sale of flags. The mayoress (Lady Bruton) took charge of the fund. At the event, there was also a baby show as well as concerts arranged by Councillor J. Embling, together with stalls, a fete and tea. In the evening, there was a dance organised.

The *Gloucester Journal* reported:

*Great interest was taken in the fancy dress parade. The competitors were marshalled at the Works and proceeded through thronged streets to the sports ground. The scene was most picturesque, costumes of all variety being worn. Britannia was represented in two or three places and there were representations of the Allied nations. Sandwich girls, costers and cowboys and Indians, riding horses, were present in numbers. Comic items, which caused much amusement, were a soldier with a soap-box pram containing an ill-assorted family of black and white 'babies' and a representation of a gentleman in evening dress and a clown, both the worse for liquor. The competitors paraded the ground and passed before the judges – Mrs Macgregor, Mrs Allen, Mrs Beech, Mrs Evans and Miss Ballinger – whose awards were as follows: Miss D Hayes (Past and Present), 1. Miss M Jones (Gloucester Wagon Co.) 2. Mrs State (Uncle Sam) 3; and Miss Davis (coster) extra prize. Originality was the principle upon which the awards were made.*

The sports events included the 100 yards men's championship, the 100 yards handicap (which included employees' sons under the age of 14 years), the open tug-of-war (which was won by the Wagon Works beating Fielding and Platt Ltd), the 1 mile bicycle handicap, the 100 yards women's championship and the 100 yards handicap (for men of 45 or over). There were many other events including a sack race, a blindfolded race and a three-legged race.

Prizes were awarded to the winners by the mayoress.

It was reported in the *Gloucester Journal* of Saturday, 20 October, that Mrs J. Ellison of 20 Tudor Street, Gloucester, had received news that her son, Lance Corporal Dudley Ellison of the Gloucester Regiment, had been badly gassed and was lying in hospital at Broughty Ferry, Scotland. Lance Corporal Ellison had enlisted in August 1914 and had been in France for thirty-one months. Before enlisting, he was employed at Messrs Price, Walker and Co.

Amongst the reports of wounded and killed soldiers, the *Gloucester Journal*, during October, carried a story about the death of Sergeant A.

Rice of the Gloucester Regiment. It read:

> *Mr. and Mrs. A.R. Rice, of Sneedhams Green, have received the news through a comrade that their eldest son, Sergt. Arthur Rice, Gloucester Regiment, has been killed in action in France. He was 22 years of age. Writing on October 7th, Sergt. W. Bundy says:*
>
> *'It is with much regret that I write you these few lines concerning Arthur's death, which has been a blow to all of us, as he was one of our best pals. I am sure he will be sadly missed by all of us, being one of the few old hands left with us. He was killed instantaneously with a piece of shell, and I was not many yards off when it occurred. When we got to him, he was dead so his pals carried him away and buried him in our cemetery by the side of his other comrades who have fallen in this terrible campaign.'*
>
> *A letter has also been received from the Rev. G.F. Helm (now at south Lambeth) in which he says: 'I was indeed sorry to hear the sad news this morning. Sergeant Rice was a real friend to me on many occasions, and I was very fond of him. He will be much missed in his company.'*
>
> *Sergt. Rice joined the Territorials in 1913, was mobilised for service when war broke out, and went to France with the battalion in March, 1915. He had been slightly wounded in the back by shrapnel and had also suffered from shell-shock; and early in the present year, he was involved in a serious train smash in France, when the train he was in ran into another which was standing on the line. Mr. and Mrs. Rice have two other sons now serving in France in the same regiment, and only about a month ago they all three met at a Y.M.C.A. hut. Before the war, Sergt. Rice was in business with his father, who is one of the firm of Abraham Rice and Sons, monumental sculptors, Southgate Street, Gloucester.*

A sitting of the Gloucester Tribunal, presided over by the mayor, Sir James Bruton, was held on Wednesday, 21 November. At the tribunal, Mr Norman gave details of the new medical categories applied to men who had been called-up for the army. Grade 1 was equivalent to general service; Grade 2 to B1 and C1; Grade 3 A and B to B2 and C2; Grade 3 A and B to B2 and C2; and Grade 3C to C3.

One of the cases heard involved two gas fitters who were deemed vital to their workplace. They were employed by the Gloucester Gas Company. It was mentioned that the company had eight other fitters but, on behalf of the company, it was pointed out that, even at present, there were too few fitters to attend to the many complaints of stove renters.

The government had urged people to use gas in order that the by-products might be available for munitions. It was stated that it would be impossibe to distribute the gas needed if the men were called up for the army. The case was adjourned so that protection cards could be applied for.

Also at the tribunal, a confectioner who carried out his business in a shop on one of the main streets of the town was given conditional exemption. His case had been before the tribunal several times before. It was stated that all attempts to sell his business had failed.

A letter appeared in the *Gloucester Journal* of Saturday, 24 November, appealing for *'knitted comforts'*. It read:

> *Dear Sir, The Director-General of Voluntary Organisations has written to say that, owing to the new conditions which have recently arisen at the front, heavy additional demands for knitted comforts for the troops will have to be met.*
>
> *I shall therefore be grateful if you will allow me to appeal through the medium of your columns to all Depots and Working Parties affiliated to our County Organisation, as to the great need which there will be in the immediate future for the increased supplies of comforts especially mufflers, mittens, helmets and socks for the use of our soldiers.*
>
> *Our Association has been asked to undertake a fortnightly order commencing on the 16th instant, to enable 'all available knitted comforts' to be dispatched overseas, and I feel sure that as soon as the necessity is known, all concerned will gladly do their utmost to help the Association to meet the urgent request of the Director-General of Voluntary Organisations.*
>
> *Yours truly, L.E. Beaufort,*
> *Chairman Glos. Voluntary Organisations.*

A letter appeared in the *Gloucester Journal* of Saturday, 22 December, entitled *'Xmas thoughts for men who shirk their duty'*. It read:

> *Sir:- 'Men wanted for the Gloucester Volunteer Regiment between the ages of 17 and 18 and those over military age.' This weekly appeal in the press meets with little or no response, and the question arises, have we got to the end of our men, are there only shirkers left? What is it they are wanted for? To prevent the possibility of things happening in England that have happened in Belgium and France, things that are almost too horrible to publish but that are officially recorded, officially photographed, and sworn to by affidavit against the time of reckoning with Germany. I give but one, but propose*

*giving a weekly dose in the hope it will reach men who ought to join, and I hope do not do so because they fail to see the immense importance of their doing so, and by lack of thinking about it, fail.*

*In Gerbevillier standing besides their graves, I studied the photographs of the bodies of fifteen old men who the Germans lined up and shot because there were no young soldiers to kill; heard the detailed story of a woman whose son was first hung to a pear tree in the garden, and when the officer and soldier had left him and were busy setting fire to the next house, she cut the rope, revived the strangled youth, only to find the soldiers had returned, and while the officer held her hands behind her back, his assistant poured petrol on the son's head and clothes, set fire to him, and while he staggered about a flaming torch, they shrieked with laughter. When they had burned all the houses and retreated the next morning, the Prefect of Lorraine reached that Gethsemane and photographed the bodies, and of women stripped and at last slain.*

*Yours obediently,*
*Marcus C. Cartwright,*
*(Sergt. Glos. Vol. Regt.)*
*Kingstanley, December 19th, 1917.*

Australian soldiers recovering in hospital praised the commandants and nurses. One commented on Christmas Day that *'Gloucester is more like an Australian city than an English one'*. He added, *'I wish the sun was a bit warmer.'*

Entertainment over Christmas included performances of *Dick Whittington* at the Palace Theatre. A preliminary run of the show on Monday, 24 December, proved hugely popular and packed houses continued over the Christmas period. The title role was taken by Miss Ray Barry as the principal boy and the show included comedians Mr Harry Ellis and Mr Will Budd as Idle Jack and Sarah the Cook. The *Gloucester Journal* reported:

*The cat, the great delight of the children, is fine, as also is the cow. A feature of the panto is the tumbling performance of 'The Five X Rays,' who caper about in an extraordinarily vigorous manner. The party includes a most peculiar dwarf, who takes a full share in the general banging around.*

Meanwhile, topping the bill at the Hippodrome was Leslie Elliott, *'the girl at the piano'*. Her repertoire included a new song, *It'll be nice to get back home again*, as well as an old favourite, *One never Knows, does one?* The newspaper described her as *'charming and vivacious as ever'*.

*Chapter Five*

# 1918 – The Final Blows

On Monday, 7 January, a fire broke out at the new paper factory at the docks belonging to Messrs Powell, Lane and Co. The fire brigade were alerted by a millhand working at Priday and Metford's mill. The brigade quickly put out the fire and Superintendent Johnson said that the fire had been started in the boiler house, caused by sacking used to wrap around the steam pipes. Because of the quick intervention, the damage only amounted to a few shillings. The superintendent issued a warning to the citizens of Gloucester not to insulate steam pipes with sackbagging but to use asbestos instead.

Another fire broke out the next day at the premises of the Farmers' Association Ltd, Millers and Corn Dealers at Quay Street. The fire was far more serious and the lower floors of the building were already well ablaze when the fire brigade arrived. After about an hour, the fire was under control although the premises suffered severe damage with various grains stored on the first floor destroyed. The *Gloucester Echo* stated that the cost of repair would run into hundreds of pounds.

In January 1918, sugar was rationed. By the end of April, meat, butter, margarine and cheese were also rationed. Ration cards were issued and people were required to register with their local butcher and grocer. People in Gloucester joined long queues to get the most basic of foods including potatoes and many other vegetables.

The *Gloucester Journal* of Saturday, 26 January, reported on the latest Gloucester County Petty Sessions. Three cases were heard

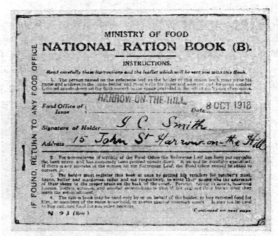

**A ration book and coupons. Sugar was rationed in January 1918 and by April, meat, butter, margarine and cheese were also rationed. Rationing became a way of life and much was in short supply.**

**Shopping in wartime. With food rationed, women and children formed long queues, overseen by policemen, to purchase whatever was available. Basic foods like meat and cheese were all in short supply.**

and reported in the newspaper:

*Hilda Russell, 4 Hatherley Street, Cheltenham, was summoned for stealing a pair of shoes valued at 12s., the property of Annie Pinchin, 3 Cotswold View, Churchdown, on December 17th. The latter, who is employed at a filling factory, stated she put her shoes under her peg as usual in the changing room before going into the danger area on the day mentioned. Later, she returned and found them gone. She watched for several days, and on January 16th saw*

**Tom Wiltshire in Italy in 1918.**

*some goloshes under defendant's peg but no shoes, and obtaining permission of the shifting house attendant to search defendant's clothes, she found the missing shoes (produced) wrapped up in defendant's coat. She saw defendant the previous evening, when the latter owned up to taking the shoes and said she was sorry. P.C. Gwinnell stated he had interviewed defendant, who admitted the theft. Defendant, who said she had no father, and supported a crippled mother, and couldn't afford to buy shoes, was bound over in the sum of £10 for six months, the chairman saying that stealing from a comrade was a disgraceful thing.*

*George Brooks, 127 New Street, was found to be in possession of one match in a box when within the danger zone of a munitions factory on January 12th. Warrant Officer Simons deposed to calling at defendant's house and finding defendant ill. The latter said, 'It is the job that's worrying me.' His wife was also upstairs ill. Evidence was given by the searcher, George Garness. The chairman said because of the illness of the defendant and his wife they would not send him to prison but he would be fined £5 and two months were allowed in which to pay.*

*Sarah Ann Smith, 20 Foxelms Road, Tuffley, applied under the Summary Jurisdiction (Married Women) Act for a maintenance order against John Edward Smith, of Bolton Road, Small Heath, Birmingham. Mr. Lionel Lane appeared for complainant and said defendant admitted desertion and was willing to pay £1 towards his wife's maintenance; but he asked for 25s., as defendant was in receipt of £3 a week, and in addition a pension from the Army of 11s. 3d. a week. An order of 25s was made with costs.*

At a meeting of the Gloucestershire Chamber of Agriculture on Saturday 16 February, the subject of pig-keeping was raised. The chairman said it was a most important point as there was a present shortage of pigs due to the Swine Fever Orders, which caused breeders great inconvenience, as did the high prices for, and shortage of, feeding stuffs. Mr W. Nixon suggested that pigs should be reared in all rural districts and that every school should have a pig or two. He said that if they could get children interested in pig-rearing that it would give their parents the incentive to rear them also. The *Gloucestershire Journal* reported:

*Mr H.W. Bruton also expressed the hope that the absurd restrictions now in force would be withdrawn. He had such a regard for pigs that he never met one in the street without feeling inclined to take his hat off (laughter). He believed the present shortage was due to the short-sightedness of the authorities in London.*

Meanwhile, also during February, Lipton Ltd were fined at the Gloucester City Petty Sessional Court for buying pigs at prices exceeding the price fixed by the Meat Order of 1917. After being found guilty, they were issued with a fine of 10 shillings with the chairman stating that every effort must be made to ensure the various orders issued were properly carried out.

In the *Gloucester Journal* of Saturday, 23 February, the newspaper carried its regular column under the headline *'What Women Can Make at Home'.* The article gave details of how to make *'a useful walking skirt'* and stated: *'However much we study economy, a new skirt occasionally is necessary but our skirt should be procured on the cheapest possible and most practical lines.'* The pattern was obtainable from the London Fashion Bureau, London, EC4 for a cost of 7d.

On Thursday, 7 March, a whist drive was organised by the post office to raise funds for the Red Cross Hospital. The event took place at the Northgate Mansions and 336 players took part, which resulted in a handsome profit of £23 11s 6d. The money went towards supplying No 32 Red Cross Hospital with five new surgical beds, which were presented to the commandant of the hospital on the following Wednesday.

A letter appeared in the *Gloucester Journal* in March about the shortage of scout leaders due to the war. It read:

*Dear Sir, During the war, it has been found more and more difficult to discover suitable scoutmasters for the existing troops in the county, to replace those who have been called up. This difficulty has prevented the formation of new troops; but after the war this will all be changed. There will then be very large numbers of the right sort of men, who will be anxious to carry on and extend the movement. I write now to say that we in Gloucestershire are already laying our plans for a forward movement the moment peace is declared. By way of preparation, we want mothers or wives or sisters of soldiers who might become scoutmasters to mention the matter to them, and to let us know of any promise or offer of service they may receive; and besides the soldiers, there must be many others who are at present too busy to take up this work, but would gladly do so after the war; will these, too, enter their names upon the waiting list?*

*Everyone agrees that there are few, if any, movements of more importance to the welfare of the young men of the country than that of the Boy Scouts Association, and this must be my excuse for trespassing on your space. As I am expecting shortly to go to France, I shall be glad if replies be addressed to the County Secretary, the Rev. C. H. Fox Harvey, Grove Court, Upton St. Leonards, Gloucester, who will send literature and information explaining the movement to anyone interested.*

*Yours faithfully,*

*J. D. Birchall, Capt.,*

*County Commissioner for Gloucestershire.*

## POTATOES IN 1918.

LAST YEAR THE COUNTY OF GLOUCESTER PRODUCED **19,300** TONS OF POTATOES.
CONSUMED **69,400** TONS OF POTATOES.
DEFICIT - **50,100** TONS.

LORD RHONDDA and Mr. PROTHERO appeal to every man who has a farm, a garden, or an allotment to

## PLANT MORE POTATOES

and make the County **SELF-SUPPORTING**.

**An advert which appeared in local newspapers during March 1918, encouraging people to plant more potatoes and make the county self-supporting.**

On Saturday, 21 April, a concert was held by the Filling Factory. There was an excellent audience at the Corn Exchange, which included the mayor and mayoress. The concert was held in order to benefit the Men's Benevolent Fund. Mr J. Mcgregor acted as chairman.

The *Gloucester Journal* reported:

> *Mr Mcgregor, during an interval in the programme, explained that owing to the number of men employed at the factory being comparatively few, and those mostly 'old crocks,' it was necessary, if the fund was to be of real benefit to the men in times of sickness, to augment it, and the very enjoyable concert arranged for that evening was one of the chosen means.*

The performing artistes were all, in some way, connected to the factory. Songsters were many with Mr S.M. Willey and Mr J. Maybrey giving violin and harp duets. Miss Franklin's monologues were well-received, as was Mr A. Stopford's 'absurdities'. The concert ended with a sketch, which was entitled *The Imposter*. The newspaper reported that a popular feature was the mystery prizes, which were awarded to the holders of the winning tickets.

On Wednesday, 24 April, the monthly meeting of the Gloucester City Council witnessed the election of the first lady councillor. Miss Edith Sessions, the new councillor for Barton ward, came from a well-known Gloucester family and her late father (Mr Jesse Sessions) had once been the mayor of the city.

At a council meeting towards the end of April, reference was made to the Board of Trade and the Lighting, Heating and Power Order of 1918. It had been suggested that a temporary discontinuation of street lighting should be tried. Councillors agreed that all street lighting should be discontinued between 15 May and 15 August, unless the police specifically requested it. The *Gloucester Journal* reported:

> *Mr Bell urged that the economy of coal consumption effected by the discontinuance of street lighting would be far outweighed by the considerations affecting public morality, and in future years they would come very much to regret it.*
>
> *Mr. Made, speaking from his patrol experience as a special constable, saw no objection to the proposed course, and pointed out that it only affected the main streets. The side streets were permanently darkened, and therefore any occasion for immorality to which Mr. Bell referred was not a new factor. There was very little traffic in the city after 9pm, and was practically confined to the exodus from public gatherings and entertainments, which in summer months ended in daylight, and to the exodus from public houses.*
>
> *Mr. Colwell said that they had no public lighting in the country and no immorality, unless it was imported from the towns.*
>
> *Alderman Estcourt, in reply, said the Chief Constable had approved the discontinuance of the lighting.*
>
> *The minute was confirmed.*

On Wednesday, 8 May, a soldier appeared at the City Petty Sessions charged with desertion and alleged false pretences. Thomas Bennett, of no fixed abode, was accused of obtaining £11 in money by false pretences from Mrs Maria Hales of 2 Raglan Terrace, Gloucester. He had told his second cousin, Mary Beatrice Hales, that he was going before the medical board to get his discharge. He said he had £100 coming to him. She said she was walking with him in Southgate Street when a car pulled up and the accused had a conversation with the driver for several minutes. He told her afterwards that a post had been offered to him for £4 a week by Sergeant Major Price and that he needed money for expenses. She then contacted her mother-in-law, who subsequently lent him £5. He later asked for more money and obtained a further £3 from Mrs Hales. However, no job had been offered to him and neither was he receiving money after being discharged. He admitted to lying and the matter was put in the hands of the police.

Sergeant Major Price, the labour officer for the county of Gloucestershire, said that while in a motor car, the accused had hailed him and he recognised him as being formerly in the Dragoon Guards in Canterbury. He had promised him no work and had not seen him since 1914.

When arrested, Bennett admitted to being a deserter from the Royal

FASHIONS FOR WOMEN IN WAR TIME

THE " SERVICE " UNIFORM
WITH BARBED WIRE TRIMMING AT THE FRONT

**A humorous postcard showing fashions for women in wartime. This one shows a dress complete with barbed wire on the front. It was drawn by popular cartoonist Reg Carter, who also later drew strips for The Beano as well as many other comics.**

Engineers but said that whatever happened to him, he would repay Mrs Hales.

In court, the prisoner claimed he had been sent to France five times since 1914, had suffered from shell-shock and been given a gold watch by an officer whose life he had saved. He said he had failed to return to his unit in January owing to family troubles, and that he had to get money from somewhere.

The chairman of the court said the prisoner had 'got himself into a tight place', but in view of the service he had seen in the army, he would dismiss the charge of false pretences. It was decided that Bennett be handed over to the military authorities and the chairman hoped he 'would make good'.

The shortage of coal had an effect on the running of the city's trams, as reported in the *Gloucester Journal* of Saturday, 18 May:

*The Light Railways Committee of the Gloucester Corporation has had under consideration for some time, the means of effecting the reduction in the consumption of electricity required by the Government under the Defence of the Realm Act so as to involve the least possible inconvenience and sacrifice of the travelling facilities enjoyed by the public. The order is drastic in its terms, and calls for a reduction of no less than 15 per cent of the coal consumed for tramways purposes in comparison with the quantity used in the corresponding period of last year. The Government has also made strong representation on the subject of man-power.*

*The immediate steps decided upon are reduction of speed and the number of stopping places, which measures will, with the co-operation of the public, go a long way towards effecting the necessary economies. The complete withdrawal of Sunday traffic, resorted to in very many towns, is the simplest method of dealing with the matter, and may yet prove to be necessary in Gloucester, but the committee feels the greatest reluctance in deciding upon a step which must curtail greatly the opportunities for fresh air and change of scene of many of the workers who have little other time for such relaxation.*

The *Gloucester Journal* of Saturday, 22 June, reported a story under the headline *'Tragic Affair at Gloucester Infirmary'*. It read:

*John Francis Gleed (21), who assisted his father in the management of a farm at Westbury-on-Severn, was admitted to the Gloucestershire Royal Infirmary on June 13th suffering from tuberculosis. He was lying quietly in bed on Friday morning, when he suddenly sprang out, and, before anyone could get to him, ran out of the ward and jumped over the balustrade on to the yard below, a distance of 43 feet, where he was found in an unconscious condition. He was treated for serious injuries by Dr. Stanley, the house surgeon but died later in the day.*

A letter appeared in the *Gloucester Journal* towards the end of June from the mayor concerning the Women's Army Auxiliary Corps. It read:

*Sir, Many of your readers may be glad to know that I have received a letter from the Headquarters of the Southern Command, stating that it is important that additional recruits for the Q.M.A.A.C. should be raised at once in order that soldiers who are required for more active occupations may be released from their present appointments in that Command. Women employed in that branch of war work, which includes many classes of employment at varying rates of pay, are thoroughly well looked after in their various hostels, comfortably housed and well fed, and their services are greatly appreciated by the soldiers for whom they work. In order to facilitate recruiting, the Mayoress is forming a small Committee, who will be glad to hear from women (not under 18) who are willing to offer their services; or application forms and other particulars may be obtained by writing to, or calling at, the Employment Exchange, No.9 Southgate Street, Gloucester.*

*Yours faithfully,*

*James Bruton.*

*Mayor of Gloucester.*

On Saturday, 6 July, members of the Gloucester Commercial Travellers'

Association entertained sixty wounded soldiers from various Red Cross hospitals within Gloucester. The men travelled by car to Hucclecote, alighting at the association's bowling green attached to the Wagon and Horses Hotel. There, they took part in bowling competitions and a whist drive. Throughout the afternoon, music was played by the Wagon Works Silver Band.

During July, the Union Jack and Tricolour were hoisted above Gloucester Guildhall. The mayor sent a telegram to the French President which read:

> *The Citizens of Gloucester observing France's Day, and mindful of the great sacrifices and splendid heroism of the French people, earnestly pray that the complete victory of the Allies may soon bring a satisfactory and lasting peace, to be speedily followed by the restoration of the beauties and greatness of France and the prosperity and true happiness of her people.*

During August, the Gloucester Gas Light Company announced that they were to increase the price of gas by 6d per 1,000 cubic feet. They blamed the price rise on the increased cost of coal.

Several cases appeared before the Gloucester Petty Sessions on Monday, 19 August, and were reported later in the *Gloucester Journal*:

> *Charles Green, 3 Laburnham Place, Saint Bridge, was summoned by his wife, Ellen Green, for a common assault. Complainant stated that the defendant continually came home in a drunken condition, and had many times knocked her about. On August 11th, he came home drunk, and because she would not drink a bottle of beer, he struck her in the face and fought her as though she were a man. Defendant said the trouble all arose through complainant nagging at him and setting the children to defy and throw stones at him. Defendant added that he was 'sick, sorry and tired of it all.' The magistrates suggested that a separation might be desirable and adjourned the case for a week for this to be arranged.*
>
> *Clara Reece, Moor Street, Gloucester, was summoned by Florence Emily Skidmore, living in the same street, who alleged the use of obscene language. Complainant gave evidence as to the language used by defendant in the course of a row which lasted for two or three days. Complainant denied that she and her friends had a grudge against the defendant, and provoked a row by hitting her little boy. Complainant agreed that defendant went down in the street, but this was caused by her trying to dance to amuse the*

*children. Complainant's mother corroborated and admitted the row was caused by one little boy hitting another on the head with a cricket bat. Mrs. Boady also corroborated. Defendant giving evidence, said her lad was hit upon the head with a cricket bat by a lad named Jones. She complained to Mr. Jones, who said something which evoked from her the reply that she did not trouble for the Martins or the Skidmores. Thereupon, the complainant and her friends set upon her. Defendant did not, however, use any bad language, but being 'rather full,' rather than cry she sang. A fine of 10s was imposed upon the defendant.*

Other cases heard included ones against Sophie Gough for keeping a dangerous dog, and John Killminster for the theft of a George III shilling and a gold ring.

Towards the end of August, Mr Bartlett of 127 Tredworth Road received a letter from the Gloucestershire Regiment stating that his son, Corporal Percy Bartlett, was believed to have been wounded and taken prisoner. Before joining up, Bartlett had worked in the printing department of the *Gloucester Journal* and *The Citizen*.

Endless tribunals were heard in the city with the aim of forcing men into the army. Throughout September, the practise continued. One case

**A topical postcard featuring a Tommy at the Front showing a soldier protecting his rear end with the caption 'I ain't riskin' havin' me bloomin' brains blown out'. Even with all that went on around them, British Tommies still kept their sense of humour.**

involved a gardener who worked at Forthampton in the cultivation of an area that was attached to a hospital for officers. He was aged 50 and classed as 'Grade 2'. The military, represented by Captain Wood, opposed the man's exemption on the grounds that there was another man, a boy and three women employed in the garden, which covered 2½ acres. Exemption for three months was granted while the employer tried to make arrangements to release the man.

On Saturday, 21 September, the mayor unveiled a memorial stone over the grave of Private G.F. Aldridge. He described the occasion as a *'sad, yet joyful ceremony'*. Private Aldridge had died in the Gloucester County Asylum in April and was previously buried in circumstances that had upset a lot of people in the city. Many local dignitaries attended the unveiling. Mr Palmer, speaking at the ceremony, stated that: 'Private George Frederick Aldridge was a brave British soldier who fought for his country and died in an institution. This brave man, after all he had done and suffered, was through a terrible blunder, buried under circumstances which moved the citizens to indignation. Such a thing, as happened in this case, should be made impossible in future in any town or village which calls the Union Jack its flag.'

Private Aldridge's original funeral had only been attended by several wounded soldiers from the asylum, because the institution had failed to inform the proper authorities of his death, and he had been buried in the equivalent of a pauper's grave. The memorial unveiled at the ceremony consisted of a stone cross with the inscription: *'In honoured memory of a gallant British soldier, 19733 Private George Frederick Aldridge, 2nd Battalion Oxford and Bucks L.I. B.E.F., died April 26th, 1918, aged 31 years. This stone was erected by the citizens of Gloucester.'* The *Last Post* was played at the ceremony by the buglers of the Volunteer Corps.

In the *Gloucester Journal* of Saturday, 5 October, an announcement was made by Gloucester post office. It read:

> *We are asked to state that, owing to so many of the staff of the Post Office being down with influenza, the work of the various departments is being conducted under great difficulties. Those on duty, however, are doing their very best to carry on, but the public will understand that any delays which occur are absolutely unavoidable.*

Two cases of theft were heard in the Gloucester courts and were reported in the *Gloucester Journal* of 19 October. The first case involved the theft of cigarettes. Charles Herbert Sims, aged 16, a farm labourer, pleaded guilty to stealing twenty-two packets of cigarettes from the property of

THE DIRECTORS OF
# LLOYDS BANK LIMITED
desire to call the attention of their customers
and others to the advisability of investing all
available moneys in

## NATIONAL WAR BONDS
and of applying further savings in the same way.

At the Savings Bank Department small sums can be
accumulated at interest until they reach the minimum
required for purchasing WAR BONDS.

## PALACE THEATRE, GLO'STER
MONDAY, OCTOBER 21st, and During
the Week.
ONCE NIGHTLY AT 7.30.  Matinee Saturday at 2.30.

IMPORTANT VISIT OF

☞  MR. ROBERT COURTNEIDGE'S  ☜
PRINCIPAL COMPANY IN THE VERY SUCCESSFUL MUSICAL COMEDY

## MY LADY FRAYLE
From the Shaftesbury Theatre, London.

SEATS NOW BOOKING AT THE THEATRE.
Telephone 176.

**An advert for National War Bonds, which appeared in the *Gloucester Journal* of 19 October 1918.**

**The musical comedy My Lady Frayle appeared at the Palace Theatre from Monday, 21 October 1918.**

Thomas Long. The accused said he went to the house to buy cigarettes but finding no one at the shop, broke in through a bedroom window. He was sent to Borstal for three years for the crime.

Georgina Agnes White, aged 20, who worked as a domestic servant, pleaded guilty to stealing a silver locket and chain together with other articles belonging to Agnes White. She was also accused of stealing 2 shillings from Francis White. The prosecutor said it was a sad case with the accused having broken into her father's house to steal the items. The prisoner had previously been convicted in London and sent to a reformatory. On returning home she was found a job but stole from her employer and was bound over by the City Quarter Sessions. She subsequently stole from another employer and ran away. The chairman said it was a sad thing that such a young girl should steal from her father, and he sent her to Borstal for three years.

**An advert from October 1918 appealing for people to buy War Savings Certificates. Their emblem contained a swastika which, at the time, denoted auspiciousness. The advert suggests that men can save money by shaving themselves, taking up DIY and not eating in restaurants.**

**Tea & Jam**

Our local branch will be
pleased to register your name
for these important commodities, if you will take your
new Ration Book to them as
soon as received.

The finest quality of goods
obtainable, and the best possible service, will be at your
disposal.

# International Stores

THE BIG GROCERS WITH THE BIG REPUTATION

International Stores, in an
advert published in November
1918, suggested that customers
register with them to receive
jam and tea. Ration books were
also required.

Adverts for Cadbury's cocoa and
chocolate and for Bovril which
appeared in the *Gloucester Journal* of
2 November 1918.

The *Cheltenham Chronicle* of
Saturday, 19 October, reported the
death of an Australian soldier in the
city. The funeral took place at the
cemetery on the previous Monday
afternoon of Private Hilder, Australian
Forces, who died at the Great Western
VAD Hospital on the Thursday before.
The funeral was attended by Mrs C.
Lee-Williams (commandant), several nurses, and a number of wounded
Australian soldiers. A firing party from the VTC under Sergeant J.E.
Mott fired the customary three volleys over the grave.

On Saturday, 2 November, the *Gloucester Journal* reported on a
rumour that was circulating the city. The article read:

*The Mayor said that he thought it was his duty to take the*
*opportunity of referring to a report which had been spread all over*
*Gloucester, which was causing a great deal of uneasiness, and was*
*calculated to injure the traders very much indeed. It was commonly*
*reported that small-pox had broken out in the city, and in one*
*instance it was stated that the number of cases was seven. I want*
*to say, proceeded the Mayor, on the authority of the Medical*

*Officer of Health, that no case whatsoever of small-pox had taken place in the city, and I hope the press will be good enough to give publicity to this contradiction of the rumour, because it is a most serious matter, that such a report should have been circulated. It appears, from what I can make out, to have arisen in this way: Some people were discussing the prevalence of influenza, and somebody is supposed to have said, 'It's almost as bad as the epidemic of small-pox!' As far as I can trace it, that is the origin of the rumour. You have the assurance of the Medical Officer of Health – and you could have no better authority – that not a single case of small-pox has occurred in Gloucester, and we all of us hope, most sincerely, that nothing of this sort will take place. (Hear, hear.)*

*With regard to the influenza, he (the Mayor) had been supplied by the Medical Officer of Health with some figures which he thought it was desirable should be made public, in view of the very exaggerated rumours which were about. The registered deaths from influenza for the three weeks ending October 26th were as follows: At all ages, 68; under five years, 11; between five and*

**The crowd at Buckingham Palace on Armistice Day. Thousands of cheering spectators lined the streets all over Great Britain to celebrate the end of the war.**

**Armistice celebrations showing many happy faces and much flag-waving. American flags were waved alongside British ones and everyone was jubilant that the war was finally over.**

*fifteen years, 8. Those figures, he (Sir James) thought compared very favourably with other towns. (Hear, hear.)*

When the Armistice was agreed between the Allies and the Germans, the fighting in Europe came to an end. It went into effect at 11 am on 11 November. When the news reached Britain, people throughout the land took to the streets to celebrate.

On 23 November, a children's day took place in Gloucester to celebrate the Armistice. The story was carried in the local paper:

*The procession of children, arranged by Councillor J. Embling, in celebration of the signing of the Armistice, took place on Saturday afternoon, and proved to be an unqualified success. This was by no means the first enjoyable day for the children arranged by Councillor Embling, and on this occasion they supported him in a manner which must have fully compensated him for all the trouble he took to give them pleasure. Shortly after 1pm streams of children might have been seen proceeding from all parts of the city towards Kingsholm Football Ground, where at 2pm, they were marshalled in procession, and the judges commenced their onerous task of selecting from dozens of Charlie Chaplins the best imitators of that renowned film comedian; the best fancy and comic dresses and costumes amongst hundreds of competitors; the best decorated cycles; and the most ear splitting tin kettle and bucket band.*

*The task accomplished, the procession started upon its tour of the city streets, and it is no exaggeration to say that the interest evinced in the procession on the part of the general public was as keen as in any event which has marked the signing of the Armistice. It is estimated that there were about 4,000 children of all ages in the procession. All were either dressed in fancy costume or else carried flags or streamers. The variety of costume and make-up was noteworthy, and extended from boys with streaks of black upon their faces to gaudily bedecked n\*\*\*\*\*s and cleverly got-up grandmothers and grandfathers. Amongst the principal features of interest, the Kaiser was an easy favourite. Dressed up in uniform and helmeted in the approved German style, he was dragged around the city with a thick rope around his neck by a Tommy, while another soldier with dummy rifle and bayonet, followed and prodded him every time he lowered his hands from the 'Kamerad' position. A motor lorry, beflagged and carrying a tableaux representing a Red Cross Hospital with nurses and patient complete was next in favour and the prize tin band was in the* *running. There were, however, many comic costumes which caused a good deal of amusement. There were three bands, the first a tin trumpet band composed of lads from one of the elementary schools, the juvenile section of the Salvation Army band, and a Scouts' bugle band, in addition to an immense amalgamated tin kettle and bucket band which brought up the rear of the procession.*

*The free concert given in the Corn Exchange on Saturday evening in connection with the children's procession arranged by Councillor Embling was a great success. The hall was crowded with a merry throng of kiddies, who enjoyed to the full the comicalities of Grogie, who was present through the kindness of the management of the Hippodrome. Other local artistes who helped the fun along were Councillor Embling, Charlie Goble and Bob Manning.*

The war had been a long and bloody one. Gloucester had played a major part in the struggle. With the war over, there wasn't a family in Gloucester who hadn't lost a son, father, nephew, uncle or brother. There were tremendous celebrations in the streets as the end of the war was announced, but the effects of the conflict lasted for years to come.

# INDEX